TA[...]
SEEDLIN[...]

A Catalog of Cotyledons

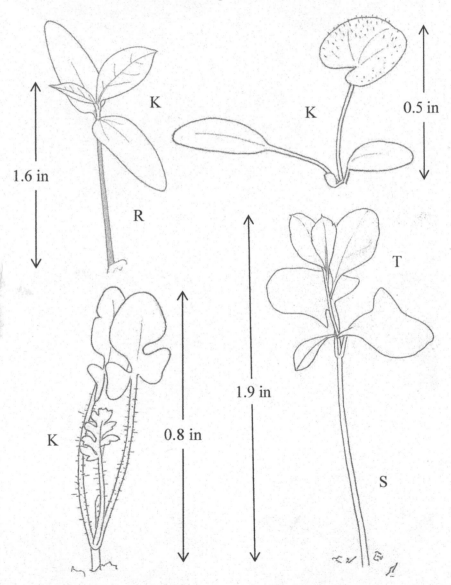

K

K

0.5 in

1.6 in

R

1.9 in

T

0.8 in

K

S

THOMAS P. TAYLOR

TAYLOR'S
SEEDLING DRAWINGS

A Catalog of Cotyledons

Thomas P. Taylor

Illustrated by
Thomas P. Taylor

2022

CONTENTS

NOTE

Seedlings are listed alphabetically by their scientific Latin family name. Then by their genus name. While checking the latest scientific classification I found that some family names still have an alternate name. Such as Asteraceae and Compositae. Or Sapindaceae and Aceraceae. I used the names currently being redirected to on Wikipedia.org, a free online encyclopedia. All the plant common names are listed in the index.

INTRODUCTION

Soon after I purchased my first home, I was faced with the task of landscaping my first lawn. If I had only known then what I was soon to learn I may have considered a gated community. Although the price was right the lawn had been neglected for many years. It would have been difficult to find a lot that had a greater number of weeds growing on it. It would be unfair however not to give some credit to the previous owner for introducing a large population of traditional garden plants. Also adding to the yard's diversity of plants was its location downwind of a flood plain of the Delaware River.

Specimen plants always provide a fascinating alternative to those that are commonly offered by the local big box stores. With this concept in mind, I began searching for the plants that I would incorporate into my landscape. During a tour of Pennsylvania's Longwood Gardens, I saw many interesting plants that would have been nice to grow, but I soon found out that many of them were varieties or hybrids not readily available at the time. I began to pocket the fruits from many of these plants so that I would have something green to see during the cold winter months in New Jersey. Even though I did not realize it at the time this was the beginning of my obsession with seeds.

I studied several good books to learn the techniques used to germinate various seeds. This is when I found out that I was not likely to see anything green very soon for almost all the plants in my temperate zone needed to be pre-treated to overcome a variety of germination inhibitors. After some research I concluded that the safest way for me to germinate seeds was to plant them outside in a prepared bed of soil. For the most part this method worked out well, except for one little problem. Many of the seedlings that came up turned out to be weeds. For some reason I was just as intrigued with these weeds as I was with the intended plant. I found them

INTRODUCTION

to be so cute that I wanted to try and capture their humble beginnings with a drawing. This is not a new concept for you can find books that provide color photos of the more common plants. These photos did not satisfy my desire for scale or detail. Not being able to find a book that presented weed seedlings in detail, I decided to produce my own catalog of seedlings.

There did not seem to be an end to the number of new mysterious seedlings coming up from out of my seed beds. Not only did I draw these unknown plants, but also those that I intended to use in my garden. After a year or two, I had an impressive number of drawings. The yard was looking good also.

As time went on it occurred to me that I might have something worth publishing. To make things more interesting I started drawing seedlings of any piece of fruit that I could get my hands on. If some plant caught my eye while I was driving around, I would make a point to harvest its fruit someday. To increase the number of plant families within my catalog I resorted to ordering seeds from several professional seedsmen. A few of the seeds that I acquired were obtained by a special request, directed towards either a nursery, a seedsman, or the U.S. Department of Agriculture, Cooperative Extension Service.

Considering the target market for people with the same interests as myself, it was difficult for me to make the time required to produce each drawing. For art's sake, I overcame all my doubts and followed through with my original intentions to produce this catalog.

VI
GERMINATION

As much as I wanted to fill this book with pages of information on the fundamentals of seedling propagation, I did not. Copying the research done by others was not the motive that drove me to prepare this album. I simply wanted to present my collection of detailed drawings to those who collect botanical artwork. However, I would like to provide the initiated with some suggestions. You need to provide a seed with all the environmental factors that it would have been subjected to had it just been removed from the plant. To germinate the seed, you must determine where it came from and then simulate the geology, exposure, temperature, humidity, and rainfall from that region. Most of the time you will get this information from the seeds package. A good encyclopedia will also provide you with some information, but you cannot ignore the possibility of there being a microclimate.

Most plants from the temperate zone will need to be stratified. This is done by placing a seed and peat mixture in a container and then hiding it in a refrigerator for a couple of months. Seeds from the tropics usually must be planted as soon as they are removed from the plant. I found that a thin layer of sphagnum moss on top of a commercially prepared cactus soil mix is a good growing media for all the terrestrial plants in my region. Larger and hard-shelled seeds usually need to be scarified. This means that you need to file a small hole in the shell to allow for water absorption. Be sure that the germination media provides aeration, and that the temperature is consistent. There needs to be good air circulation to provide the oxygen necessary for germination and to inhibit the growth of bacteria.

It is not difficult to create an environment that will germinate a seed that's ready to sprout. You could put a prepared seed flat on top of the refrigerator and let the natural effects of day and night coax the seeds to grow, providing that you can

GERMINATION

maintain the proper moisture level in the soil. This waiting period could last a couple of months. The real problem begins when the seeds start to germinate. Some seeds will begin earlier than others and will require a different environment than the slower ones. Once the seedling emerges it is best to have the top surface of the soil on the dry side. This is rather difficult to do in a cellular seed flat. The more soil that the pot has in it the easier it will be to control. An immediate transplanting is not always the solution however for it is easy to injure the tiny plant, or its tap root, which may be longer than its sprout. The use of water and fungicide must be done carefully to encourage a deep and healthy root system. Soon the plant becomes increasingly dependent on the real world and less so on the nutrients supplied by the seed leaves.

Many of the seedlings within this catalog did not need any planning whatsoever. I merely had to transplant them from where they were born into a small pot. If there were no signs of transplant shock, I could set them up for drawing right away. Otherwise, I would have to nurse the plant back to health. When I used a premanufactured seed starter kit I could just wait until the plant was ready and then cut out the cell containing the plant to be drawn.

It was occasionally evident that a plant growing under intense sunlight does not obtain the same proportions as the same plant born in the shade. One found under the sunshine will tend to be more compact, and often have red tinted leaves and stem. Even though this happens in the wild, most propagators will provide shade for the seed beds to protect the emergent plants from burning up. Whenever I could I followed this practice, and for several reasons. One is that most of us will follow the procedures developed by professionals. Another reason is that it enhances the variations that distinguish one plant from another. Of course, the main reason was that the plants were larger and easier to see and draw. When you look at some of these plants you might suspect that they were given no light at all. These will most likely be the vines. There is also a tendency for tall, fast-growing plants to develop a lazy hypocotyl. The stem below the cotyledons. Do not panic because this is just their way of creating a flexible connection to the earth which will allow the plant to bend in the wind without breaking.

For my drawings, I selected the best representative of the lot and introduced it to a sixteen-hour day period under a high-powered incandescent light. After a time of one to ten days, the specimen would be ready to draw.

DRAWING

I did not use photography or photographs of any kind to draw these sketches. I set the plant up in the position I needed it and began sketching the plant on paper much like a painter would on his canvas. I started with light lines to refine everything. I used a straight edge held up in front of the plant, to transfer any angles down to the paper. I used the top of a pencil and a ruler to measure and scale up distances. A magnifying glass was necessary to enlarge any obscure details of the seedling. Sometimes this took so long that the plant began to bend towards the light, changing the angles. Once done the plant could be put away. I would usually take a long break before defining the sketch with dark lines. I had to keep a sharp point on a rather hard lead. A sharpening pad was used to shape the pencil point.

For my earliest drawings, I used a rough unfinished drawing paper. Digitizing these produced a light gray background, which had to be removed when editing the scans. Later, I started using a smoother whiter drawing paper. My HP ENVY Pro 6458e scanner, set at 1200 DPI resolution, even captured pencil imprints remaining from erased line work.

The scanned images were touched up using Paint.net.

Each book page was produced using Microsoft Word.

LEGEND OF COLOR SYMBOLS

B = Burgundy

C = Coral Pink

F = Forest Green

G = Green tea

H = Hickory

K = Kelly Green

P = Light Red

R = Ruby Red

S = Desert Sand

T = Teal Green

W = White

Y = Light Yellow

COLOR NOTE

Depending on the ambient lighting or temperature, a pink color can become a darker red. A dark green leaf can become lighter. For these reasons, I am just referring to the colors which have been printed on the back cover. A stem with two or three colors will transition gradually between them.

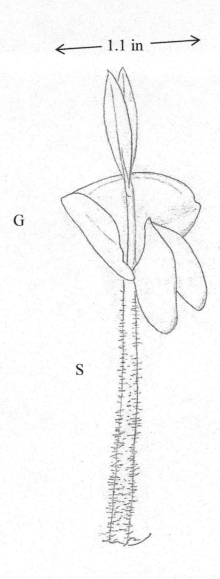

←— 1.1 in —→

G

S

Black mangrove
(Avicennia germinans)

G, green tea; S, desert sand.

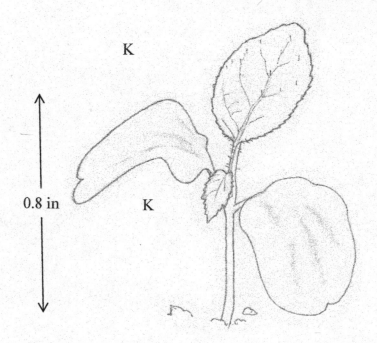

Chinese gooseberry, Kiwi
(Actinidia deliciosa)

K, Kelly green.

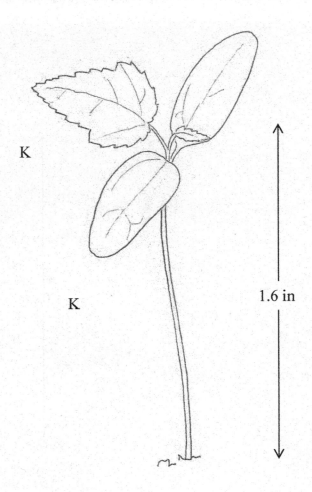

K

K

1.6 in

American storax, American sweetgum
(Liquidambar styraciflua)

K, Kelly green.

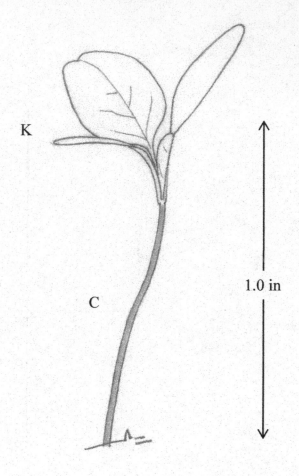

Red-root amaranth, Redroot pigweed
(Amaranthus retroflexus)

C, coral pink; K, Kelly green.

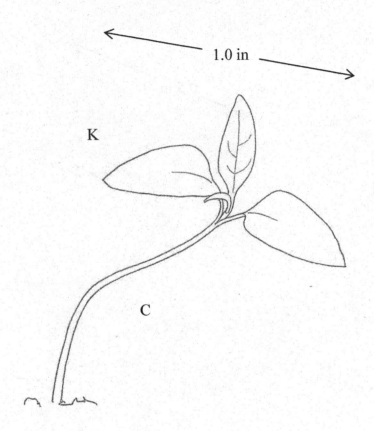

1.0 in

K

C

Plumed cockscomb, Silver cock's comb
(Celosia argentea)

C, coral pink; K, Kelly green.

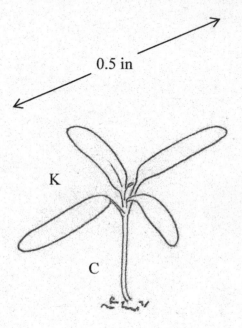

0.5 in

K

C

Goosefoot, Lamb's quarters, Melde
(Chenopodium album)

C, coral pink; K, Kelly green.

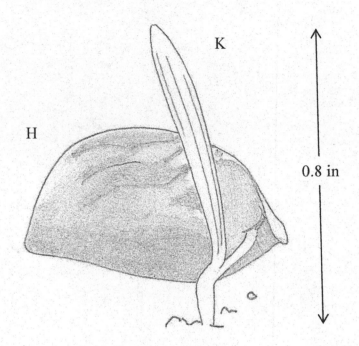

K

H

0.8 in

Amaryllis
(Hippeastrum reginae)

H, hickory; K, Kelly green.

ANACARDIACEAE

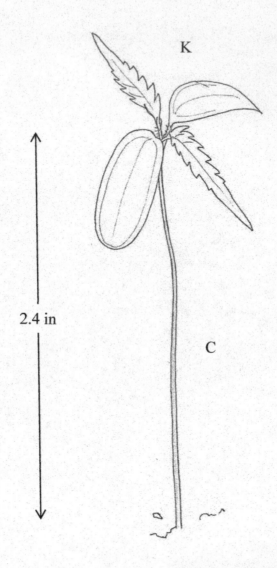

Smooth sumac, Upland sumac, White sumac
(Rhus glabra)

C, coral pink; K, Kelly green.

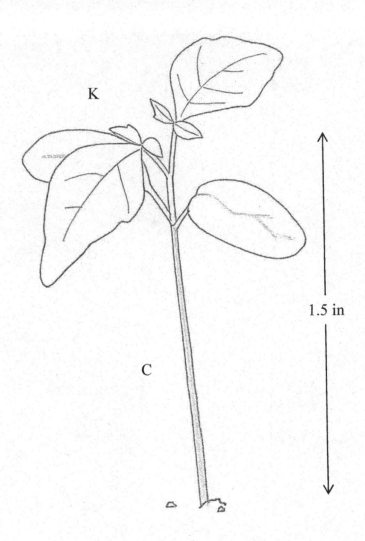

K

C

1.5 in

Poison ivy
(Toxicodendron radicans)

C, coral pink; K, Kelly green.

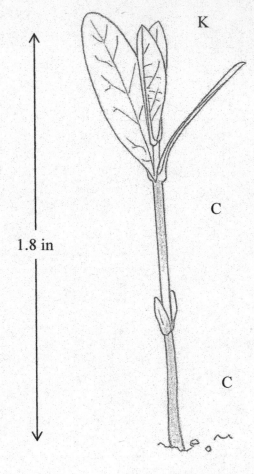

A root sprout

Dogbane, Hemp dogbane, Indian hemp
(Apocynum cannabinum)

C, coral pink; K, Kelly green.

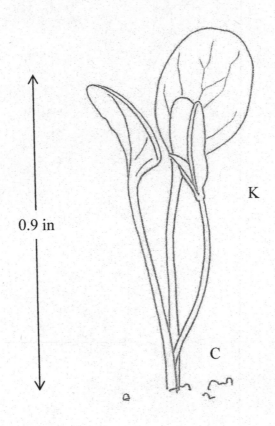

0.9 in

K

C

Butterfly weed, Pleurisy root
(Asclepias tuberosa)

C, coral pink; K, Kelly green.

APOCYNACEAE

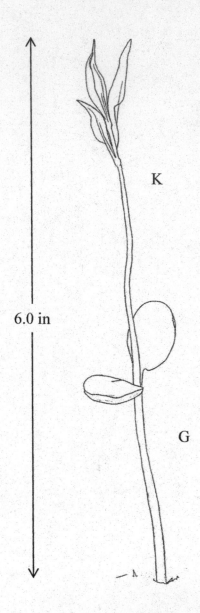

6.0 in

K

G

Lucky nut, Yellow oleander
(Cascabela thevetia)

G, green tea; K, Kelly green.

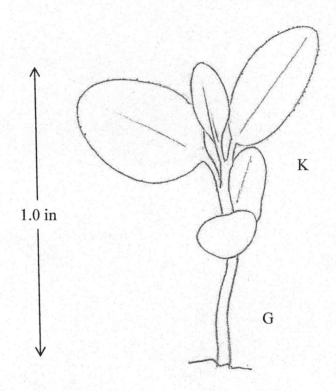

Catberry, Mountain holly
(Ilex mucronata)

G, green tea; K, Kelly green.

AQUIFOLIACEAE

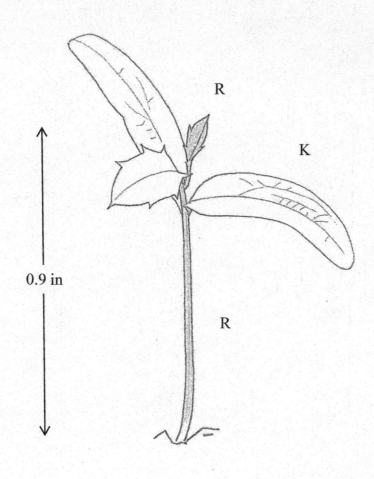

0.9 in

American holly
(Ilex opaca)

K, Kelly green; R, ruby red.

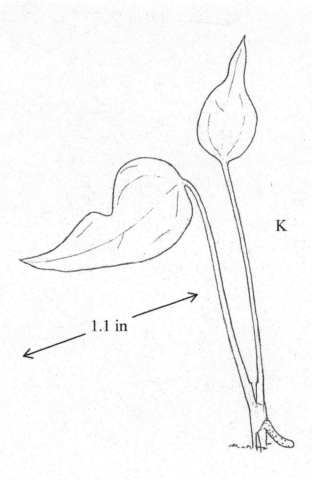

1.1 in

K

Bird's nest anthurium
(Anthurium hookeri)

K, Kelly green.

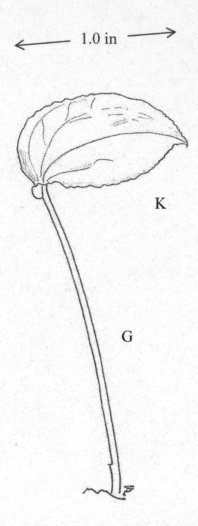

← — 1.0 in — →

Bog onion, Indian turnip, Jack-in-the-pulpit
(Arisaema triphyllum)

G, green tea; K, Kelly green.

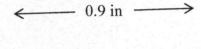

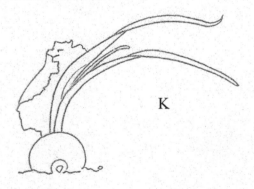

Floating arum, Golden-club
(Orontium aquaticum)

K, Kelly green.

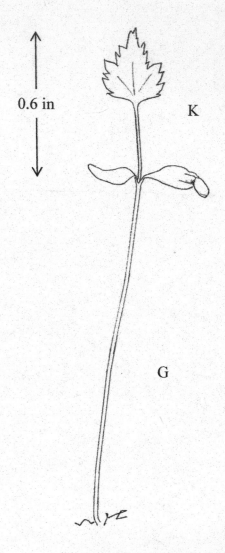

0.6 in

K

G

Devil's walking stick, Hercules' club
(Aralia spinosa)

G, green tea; K, Kelly green.

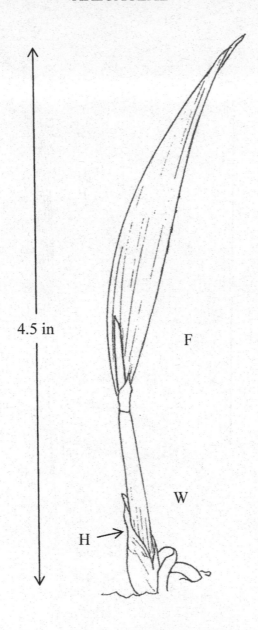

4.5 in

F

W

H →

Chilean wine palm, Chile cocopalm
(Jubaea chilensis)

F, forest green; H, hickory brown; W, white.

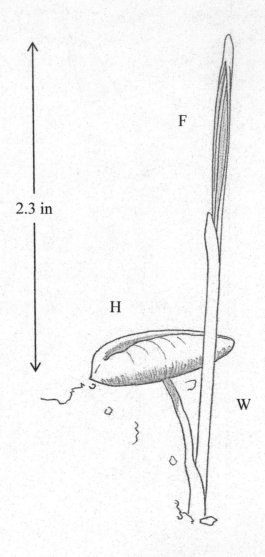

2.3 in

F

H

W

Date palm
(Phoenix dactylifera)

F, forest green; H, hickory brown; W, white.

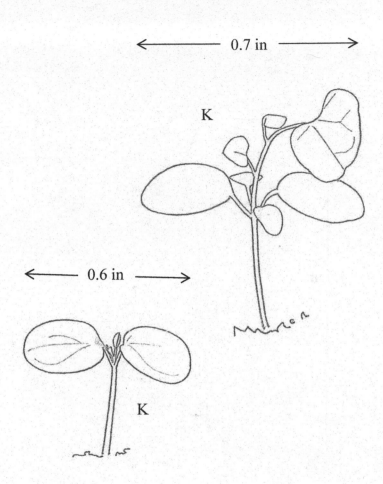

Calico flower, Elegant dutchman's pipe
(Aristolochia elegans)

K, Kelly green.

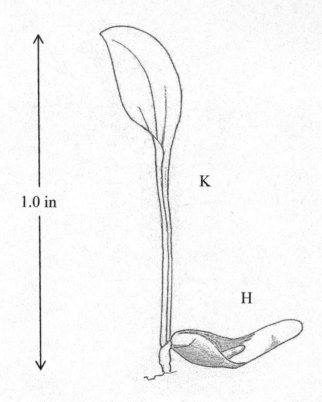

1.0 in

K

H

Hosta, Plantain lily
(Hosta sieboldiana)

H, hickory brown; K, Kelly green.

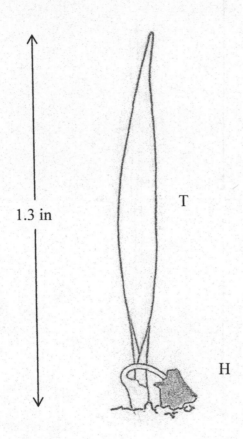

1.3 in

T

H

Adam's needle and thread
(Yucca filamentosa)

H, hickory brown; T, teal green.

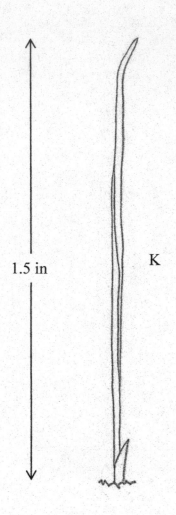

1.5 in

K

Red hot poker, Torch lily, Tritomea
(Kniphofia uvaria)

K, Kelly green.

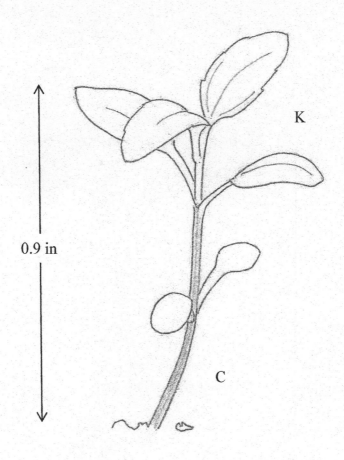

0.9 in

K

C

Richweed, White snakeroot
(Ageratina altissima)

C, coral pink; K, Kelly green.

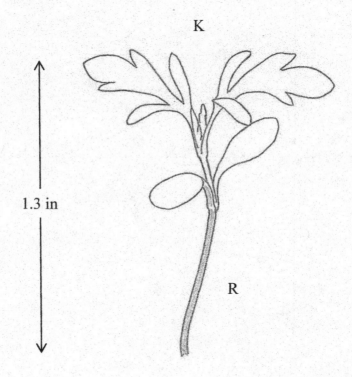

1.3 in

Common ragweed
(Ambrosia artemisiifolia)

K, Kelly green; R, ruby red.

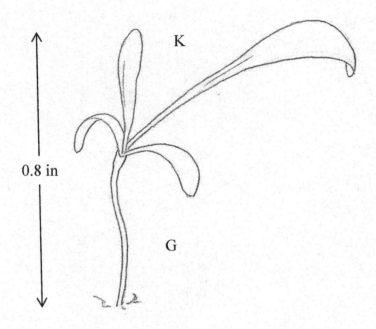

Arctic daisy
(Arctanthemum arcticum)

G, green tea; K, Kelly green.

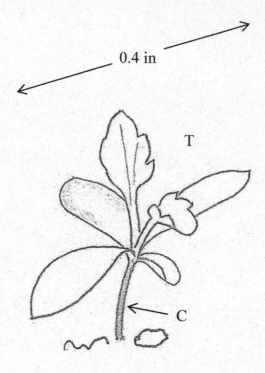

Absinthe, Mugwort, Wormwood
(Artemisia absinthium)

C, coral red; T, teal green.

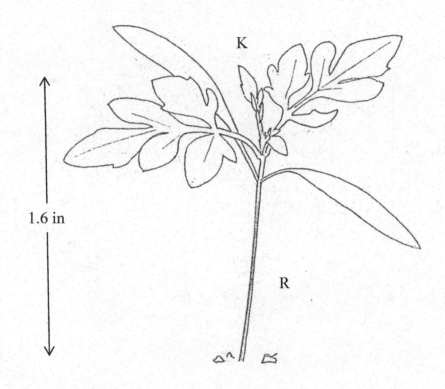

1.6 in

K

R

Beggar-ticks, Spanish needles
(Bidens bipinnata)

K, Kelly green; R, ruby red.

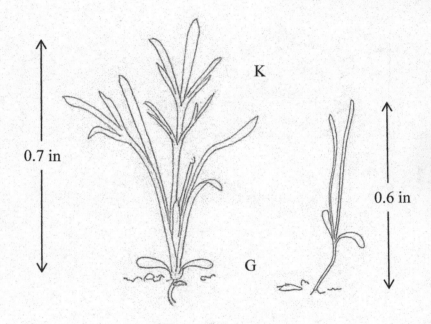

Chamomile, Roman chamomile
(Chamaemelum nobile)

G, green tea; K, Kelly green.

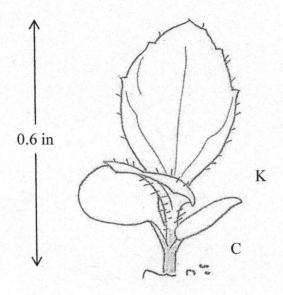

0.6 in

K

C

Fireweed, Pilewort
(Erechtites hieraciifolius)

C, coral pink; K, Kelly green.

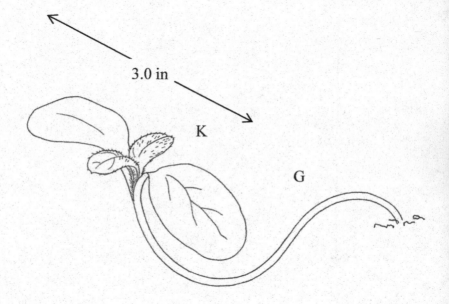

3.0 in

K

G

Common sunflower
(Helianthus annuus)

G, green tea; K, Kelly green.

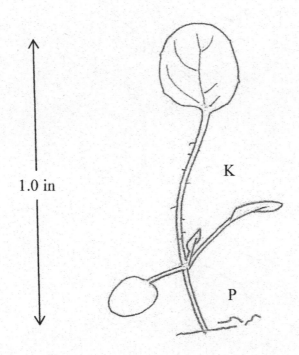

1.0 in

K

P

Common hawkweed, Yellow hawkweed
(Hieracium lachenalii)

K, Kelly green; P, light red.

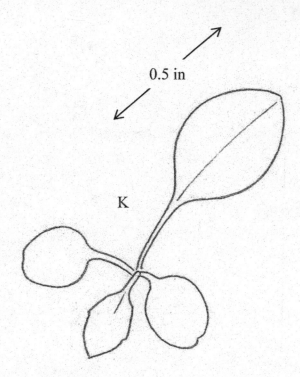

0.5 in

K

Dwarf dandelion
(Krigia virginica)

K, Kelly green.

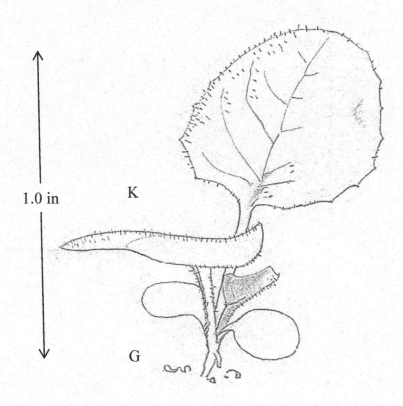

Canada lettuce, Wild lettuce
(Lactuca canadensis)

G, green tea; K, Kelly green.

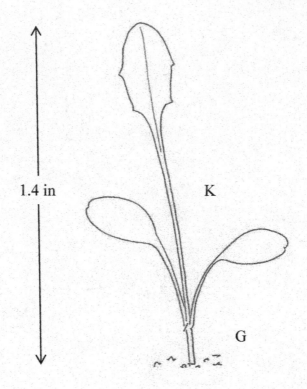

1.4 in

K

G

Common dandelion
(Taraxacum officinale)

G, green tea; K, Kelly green.

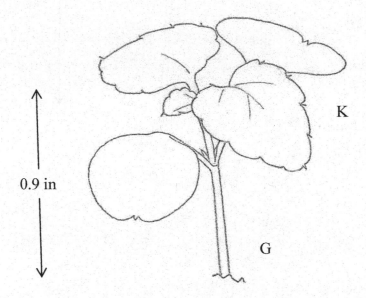

0.9 in

K

G

Balsam, Busy lizzie, Impatiens
(Impatiens walleriana)

G, green tea; K, Kelly green.

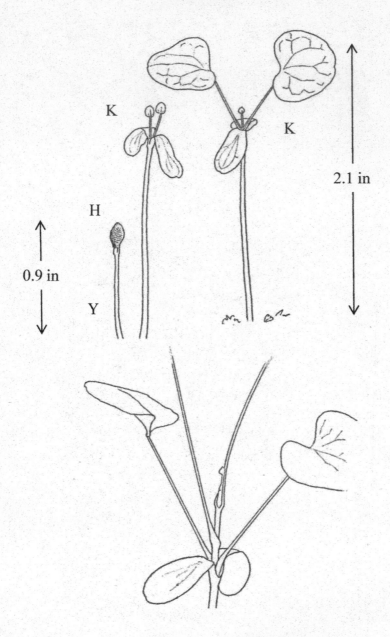

K

K

2.1 in

H

0.9 in

Y

Japanese barberry, Red barberry
(Berberis thunbergii)

H, hickory brown; K, Kelly green; Y, light yellow.

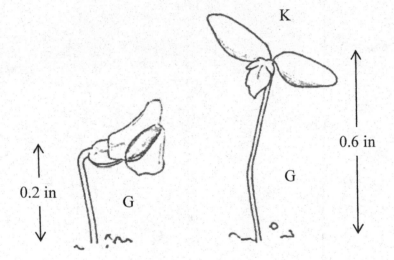

K

0.6 in

0.2 in

G

G

Gray birch
(Betula populifolia)

G, green tea; K, Kelly green.

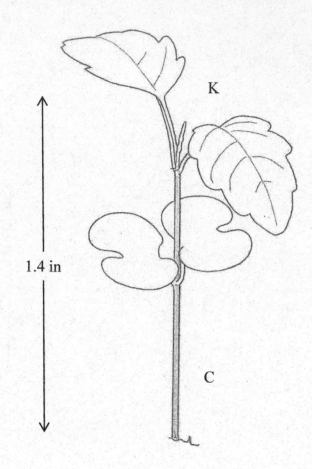

1.4 in

Trumpet creeper, Trumpet vine
(Campsis radicans)

C, coral pink; K, Kelly green.

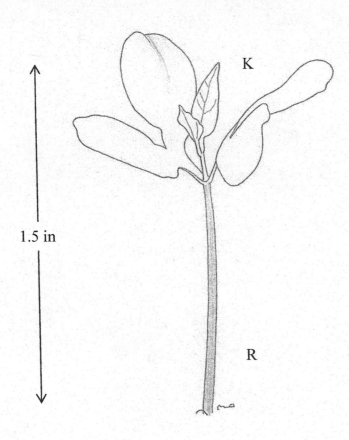

1.5 in

Cigar-tree, Hardy catalpa, Northern catalpa
(Catalpa speciosa)

K, Kelly green; R, ruby red.

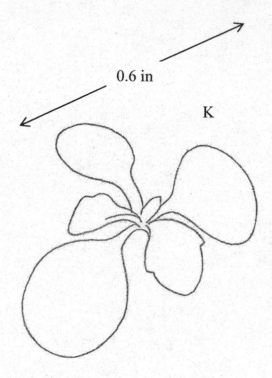

0.6 in

K

Mountain rock cress, Wall cress
(Arabis caucasica x rosea)

K, Kelly green.

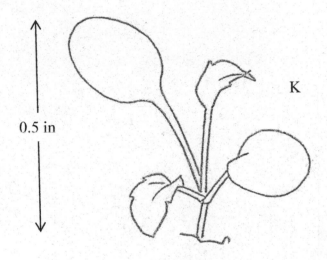

0.5 in

K

Least pepperwort, Virginia pepperweed
(Lepidium virginicum)

K, Kelly green.

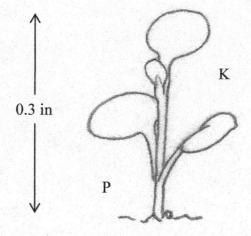

0.3 in

K

P

Watercress, Yellowcress
(Nasturtium officinale)

K, Kelly green; P, light red.

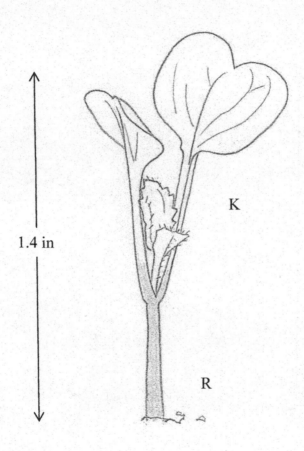

1.4 in

K

R

Radish
(Raphanus raphanistrum x sativus)

K, Kelly green; R, ruby red.

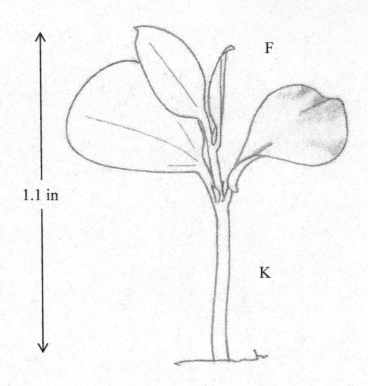

1.1 in

F

K

Fragrant sarcococca
(Sarcococca ruscifolia)

F, forest green; K, Kelly green.

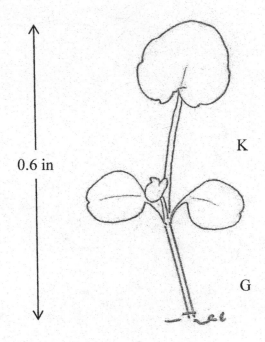

0.6 in

K

G

American bellflower, Tall bellflower
(Campanula americana)

G, green tea; K, Kelly green.

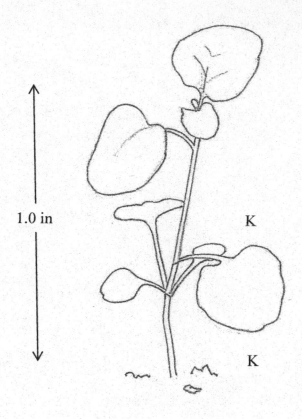

1.0 in

K

K

Clasping bellflower, Clasping venus' looking-glass
(Triodanis perfoliata)

K, Kelly green.

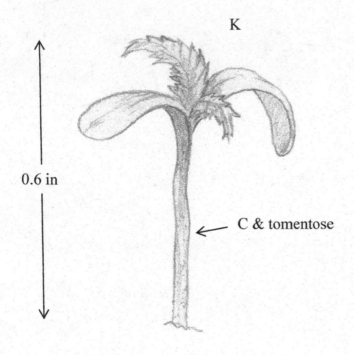

Marijuana, Hemp
(Cannabis indica)

C, coral pink; K, Kelly green.

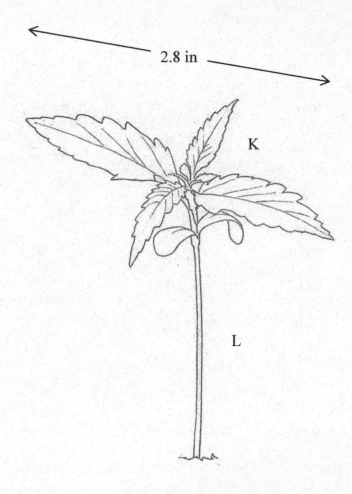

2.8 in

K

L

Hemp, Marijuana
(Cannabis sativa)

K, Kelly green; L, light red.

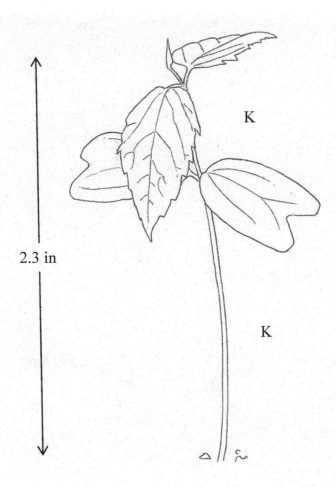

2.3 in

K

K

American hackberry, Nettletree, Sugarberry
(Celtis occidentalis)

K, Kelly green.

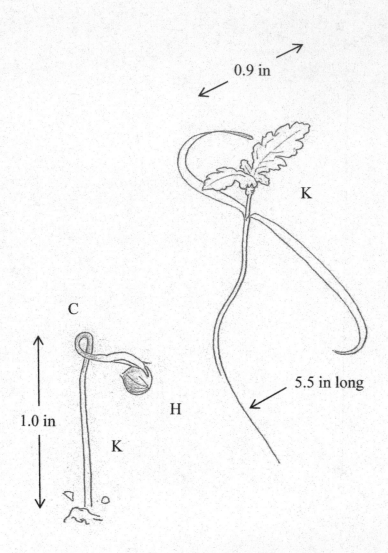

Japanese hop
(Humulus japonicus)

C, coral pink; H, hickory brown; K, Kelly green.

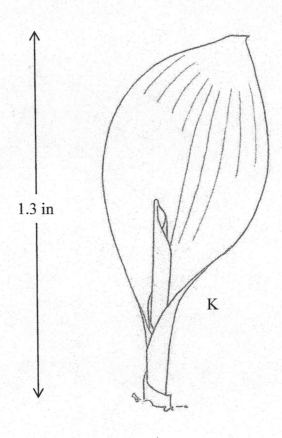

1.3 in

K

Canna, Canna lily
(Canna x generalis)

K, Kelly green.

CAPRIFOLIACEAE

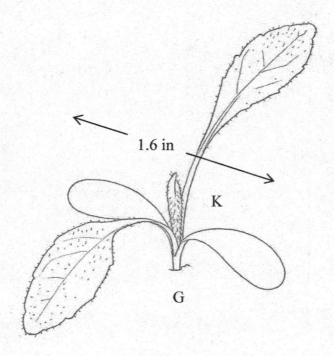

1.6 in

K

G

Giant scabious, Yellow scabious
(Cephalaria gigantea)

G, green tea; K, Kelly green.

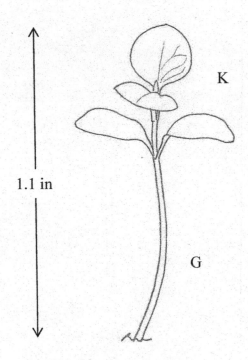

1.1 in

Japanese honeysuckle
(Lonicera japonica)

G, green tea; K, Kelly green.

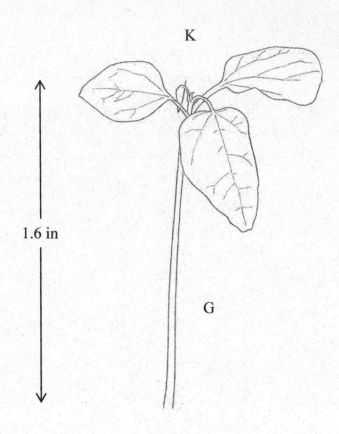

Papaya
(Carica papaya)

G, green tea; K, Kelly green.

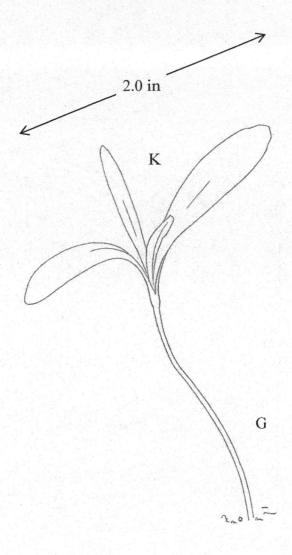

Corn cockle
(Agrostemma githago milas rose)

G, green tea; K, Kelly green.

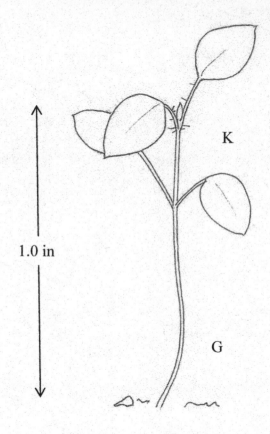

Chickenwort, Common chickweed
(Stellaria media)

G, green tea; K, Kelly green.

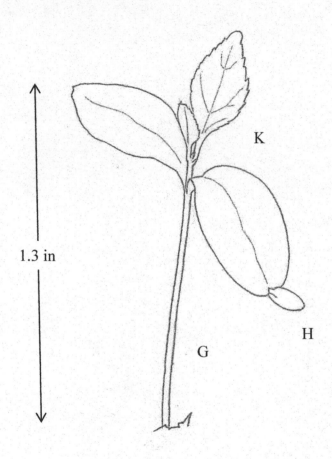

American bittersweet, Bittersweet
(Celastrus scandens)

G, green tea; H, hickory brown; K, Kelly green.

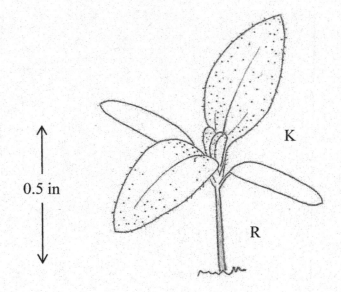

0.5 in

K

R

Sage-leaved rock-rose
(Cistus salviifolius)

K, Kelly green; R, ruby red.

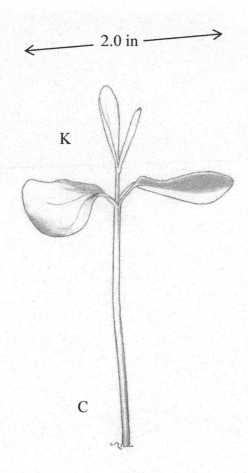

2.0 in

K

C

White mangrove
(Laguncularia racemosa)

C, coral pink; K, Kelly green

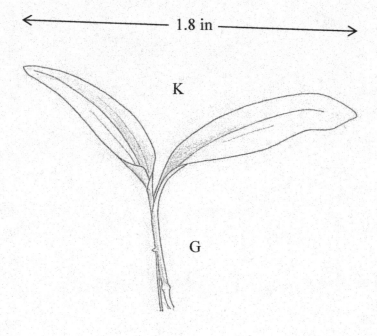

← —————— 1.8 in —————— →

K

G

Asiatic dayflower
(Commelina communis)

G, green tea; K, Kelly green

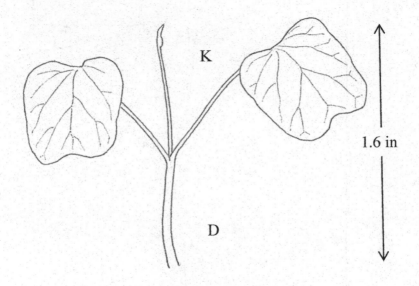

Field bindweed, Perennial morning glory
(Convolvulus arvensis)

D, desert sand; K, Kelly green

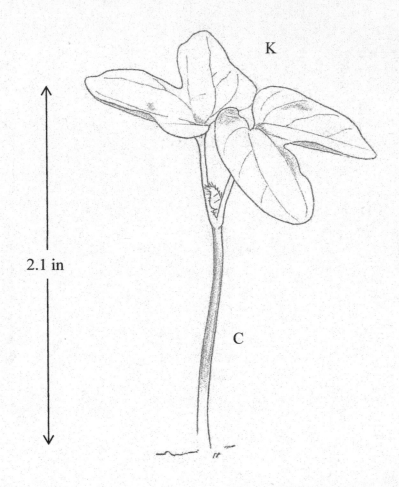

2.1 in

K

C

Ivy-leaved morning glory
(Ipomoea hederacea)

C, coral pink; K, Kelly green

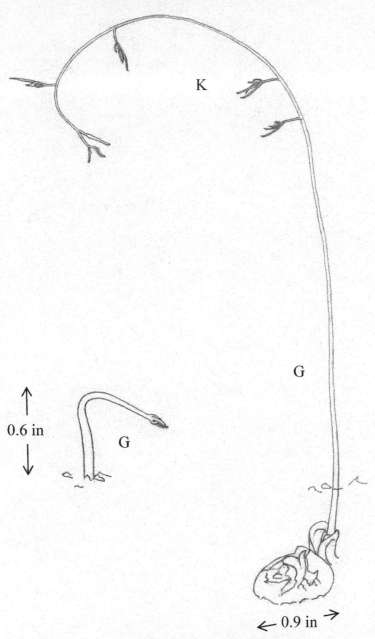

0.6 in

G

K

G

← 0.9 in →

Spanish arborvine, Woodrose
(Merremia tuberosa)

G, green tea; K, Kelly green

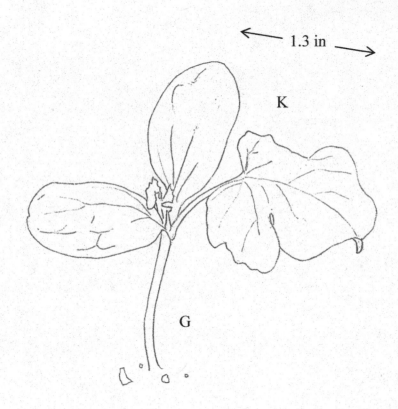

← 1.3 in →

K

G

Watermelon
(Citrullus lanatus)

G, green tea; K, Kelly green

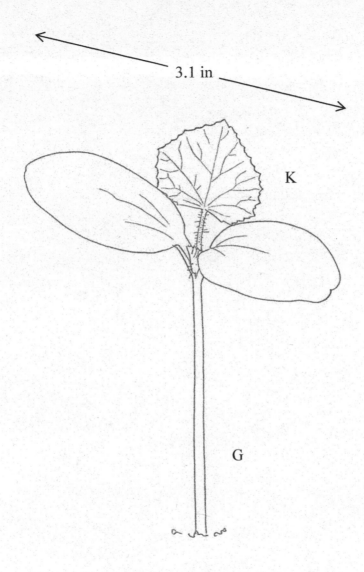

3.1 in

K

G

Cantaloupe, Honeydew, Muskmelon
(Cucumis melo)

G, green tea; K, Kelly green

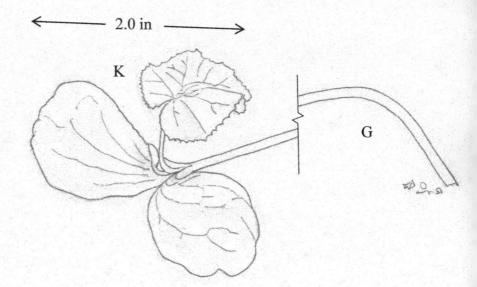

← 2.0 in →

K

G

Pumpkin
(Cucurbita pepo)

G, green tea; K, Kelly green

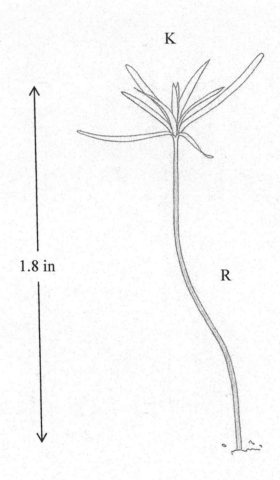

K

1.8 in

R

Eastern red cedar, Red juniper, Virginian juniper
(Juniperus virginiana)

K, Kelly green; R, ruby red

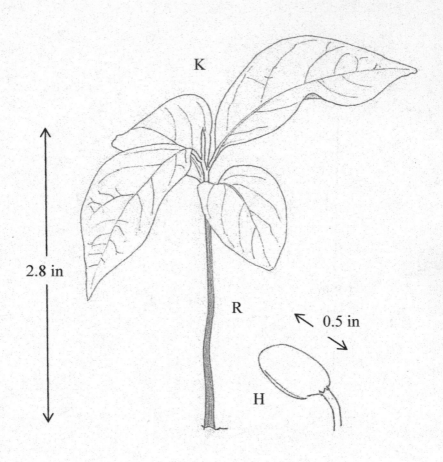

K

2.8 in

R

0.5 in

H

American persimmon, Possumwood, Sugar plum
(Diospyros virginiana)

H, hickory brown; K, Kelly green; R, ruby red

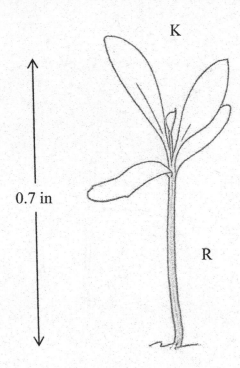

0.7 in

Bearberry, Kinnikinnick
(Arctostaphylos uva-ursi)

K, Kelly green; R, ruby red

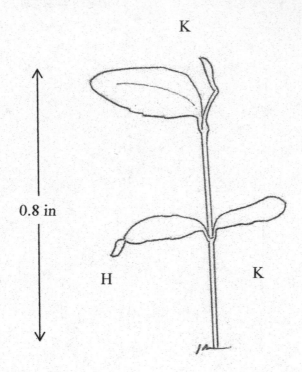

Coastal dog-hobble, Swamp dog-laurel
(Leucothoe axillaris)

H, hickory brown; K, Kelly green

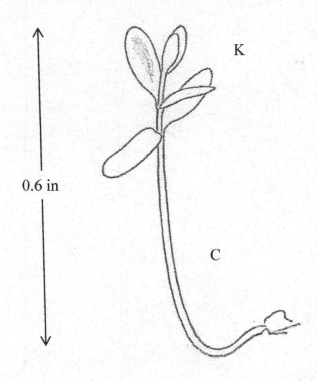

0.6 in

K

C

American cranberry
(Vaccinium macrocarpon)

C, coral pink; K, Kelly green

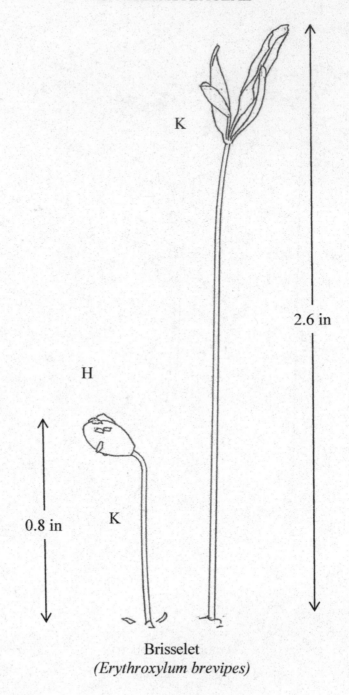

K

2.6 in

H

0.8 in   K

Brisselet
(Erythroxylum brevipes)

H, hickory brown; K, Kelly green

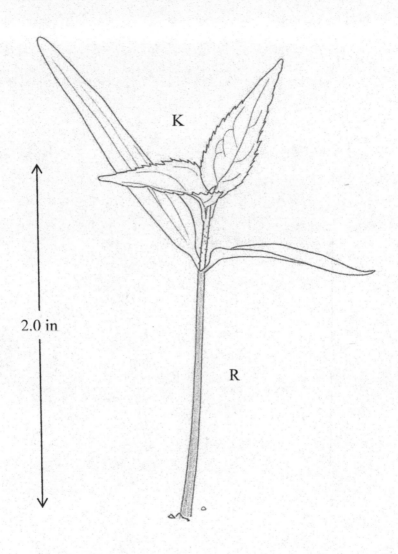

Hardy rubber tree
(Eucommia ulmoides)

K, Kelly green; R, ruby red

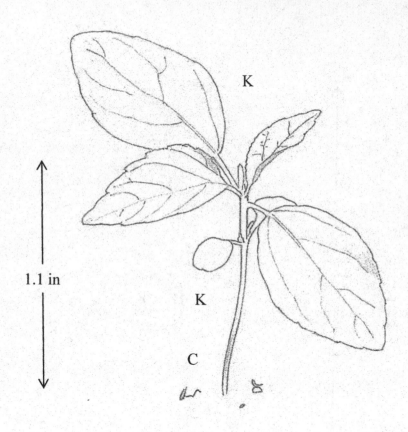

1.1 in

Three-seeded mercury
(Acalypha rhomboidea)

C, coral red; K, Kelly green

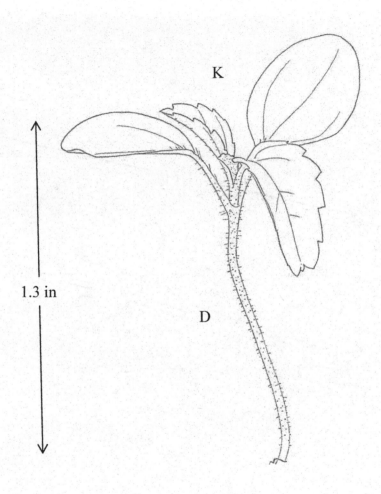

Sand croton, Tropic croton
(Croton glandulosus)

D, desert sand; K, Kelly green

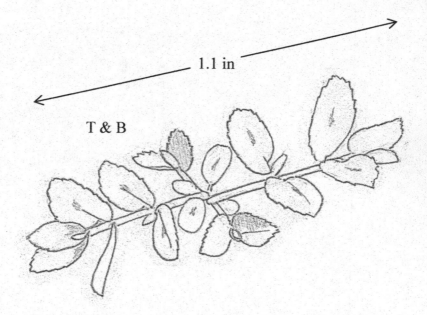

1.1 in

T & B

Prostrate spurge, Spotted spurge
(Euphorbia maculata)

B, burgundy in center; T, teal green

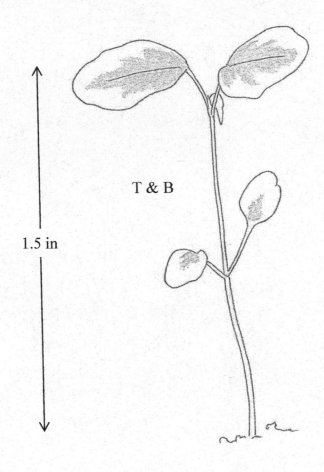

T & B

1.5 in

Flameleaf spurge
(Euphorbia x Flameleaf)

B, burgundy in center; T, teal green

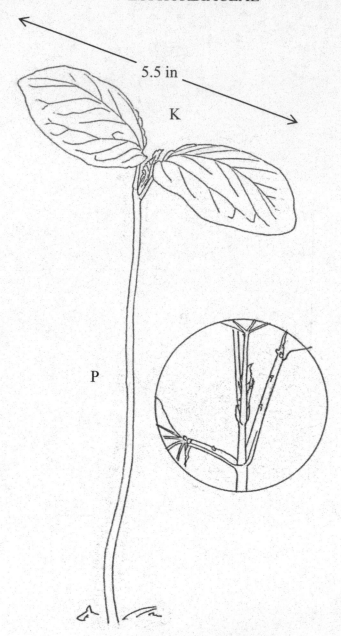

5.5 in

K

P

Castor bean, Castor oil plant
(Ricinus communis)

K, Kelly green; P, light red

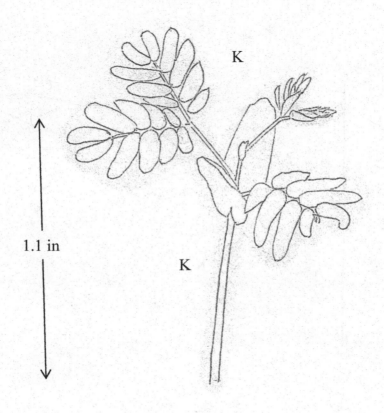

Persian silk tree, Pink silk tree
(Albizia julibrissin)

K, Kelly green

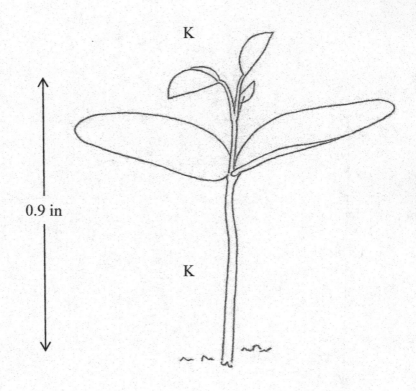

False indigo-bush
(Amorpha fruticosa)

K, Kelly green

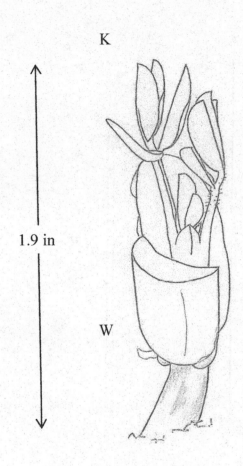

K

1.9 in

W

Goober, Groundnut, Peanut
(Arachis hypogaea)

K, Kelly green; W, white (a cutaway)

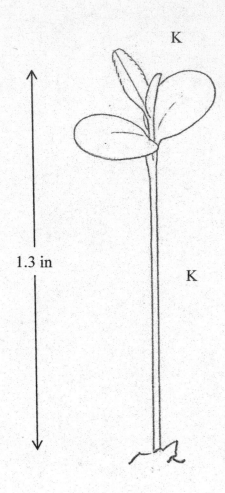

K

1.3 in

K

Mount Etna broom
(Genista aetnensis)

K, Kelly green

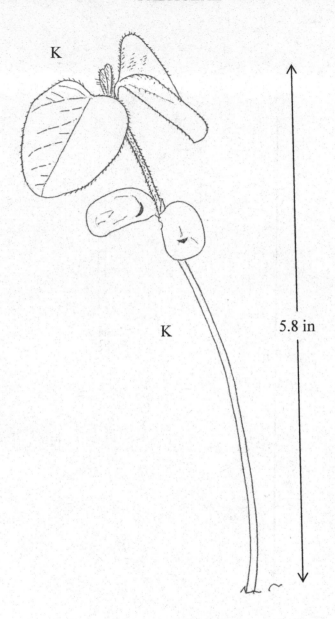

K

K

5.8 in

Soybean
(Glycine max)

K, Kelly green

FABACEAE

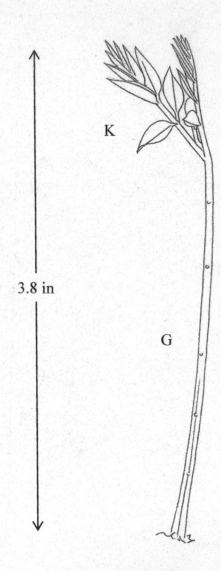

3.8 in

K

G

Kentucky coffetree
(Gymnocladus dioicus)

G, green tea; K, Kelly green

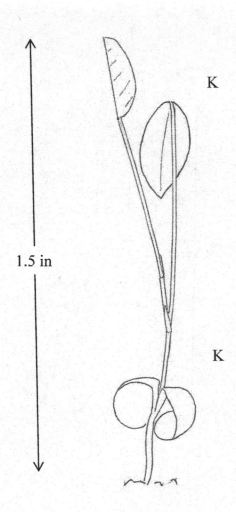

1.5 in

K

K

Alpine sweetvetch
(Hedysarum alpinum)

K, Kelly green

FABACEAE

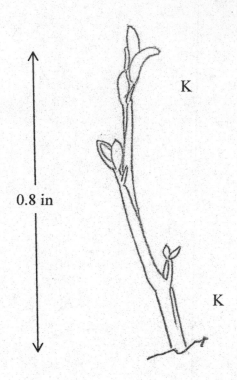

0.8 in

K

K

Everlasting pea, Perennial pea
(Lathyrus latifolius)

K, Kelly green

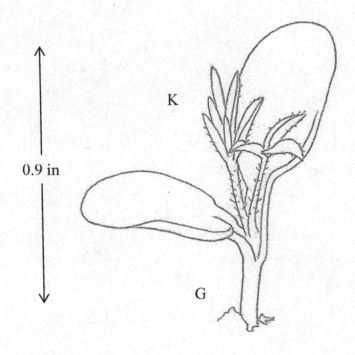

0.9 in

K

G

Tree lupine, Yellow bush lupine
(Lupinus arboreus)

G, green tea; K, Kelly green

FABACEAE

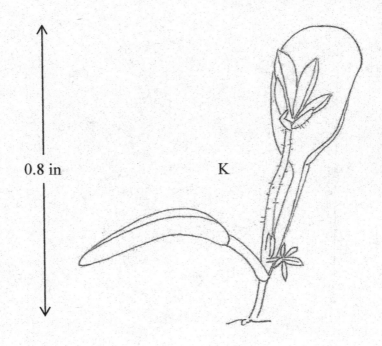

0.8 in   K

Nootka lupine
(Lupinus nootkatensis)

K, Kelly green

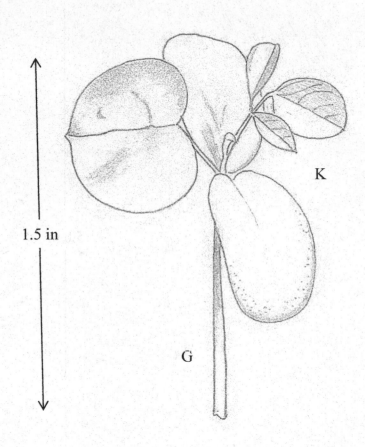

1.5 in

K

G

Black locust, False acacia
(Robinia pseudoacacia)

G, green tea; K, Kelly green

FABACEAE

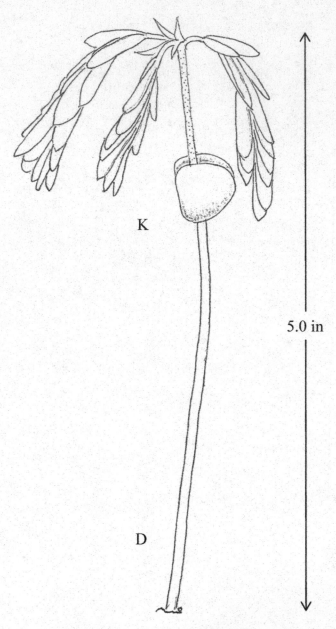

K

D

5.0 in

Tamarind
(Tamarindus indica)

D, desert sand; K, Kelly green

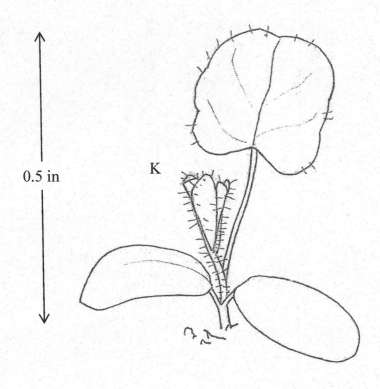

0.5 in

K

Dutch clover, White clover
(Trifolium repens)

K, Kelly green

FABACEAE

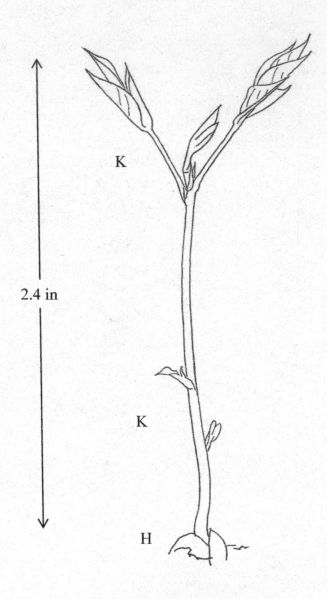

2.4 in

K

K

H

American wisteria
(Wisteria frutescens)

H, hickory brown; K, Kelly green

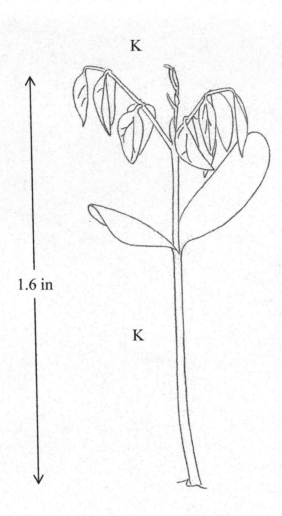

K

1.6 in

K

Chinese wisteria
(Wisteria sinensis)

K, Kelly green

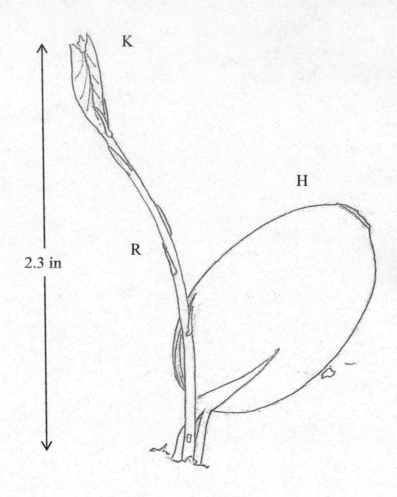

K

H

2.3 in

R

Chestnut oak, Rock oak
(Quercus montana)

H, hickory brown; K, Kelly green; R, ruby red

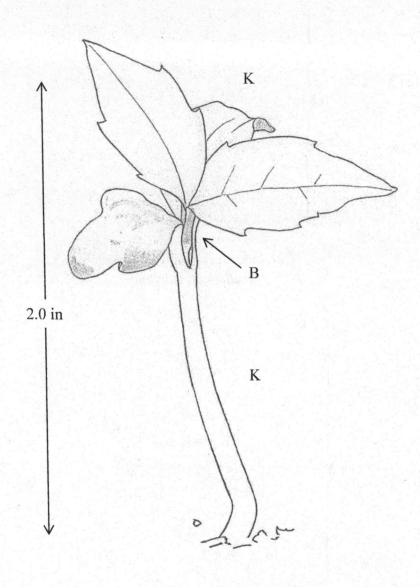

Gold dust plant, Japanese aucuba, Japanese laurel
(Aucuba japonica)

B, burgundy; K, Kelly green

GERANIACEAE

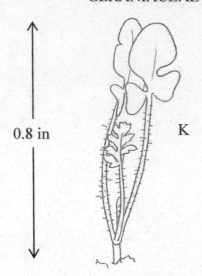

0.8 in

K

Common stork's-bill, Pinweed
(Erodium cicutarium)

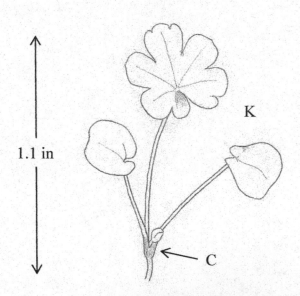

1.1 in

K

C

Carolina crane's-bill, Carolina geranium
(Geranium carolinianum)

C, coral pink; K, Kelly green

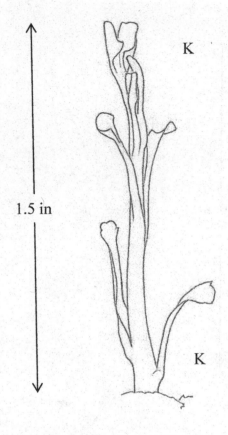

1.5 in

K

K

Hypogeal

Ginkgo, Maidenhair tree
(Ginkgo biloba)

K, Kelly green; Hypogeal, meaning below ground

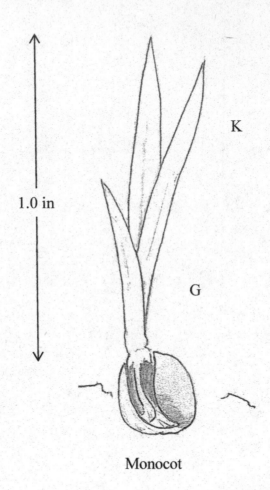

1.0 in

K

G

Monocot

Blackberry lily, Leopard lily
(Iris domestica)

G, green tea; K, Kelly green; Monocot, has one cotyledon

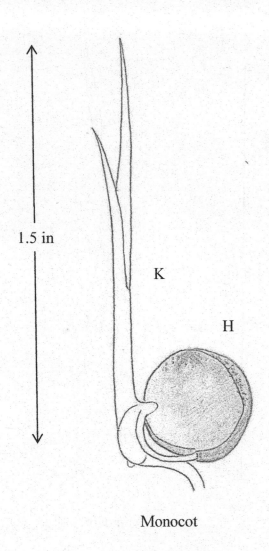

1.5 in

K

H

Monocot

Water flag, Yellow flag, Yellow Iris
(Iris pseudacorus)

H, hickory brown; K, Kelly green; Monocot, has one cotyledon

IRIDACEAE

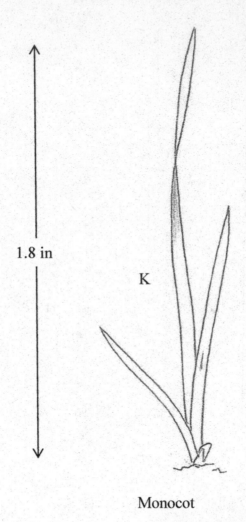

1.8 in

K

Monocot

Bristle-pointed iris, Wild iris
(Iris setosa)

K, Kelly green; Monocot, has one cotyledon

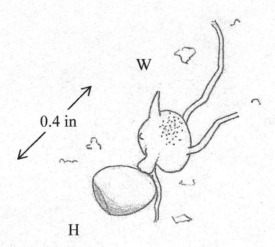

0.4 in

W

H

Bearded iris, German flag
(Iris x germanica)

H, hickory; W, white

LAMIACEAE

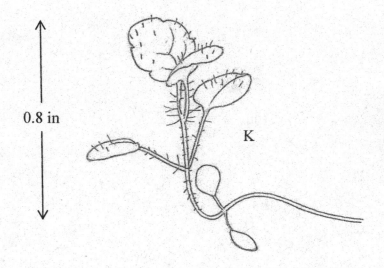

0.8 in

K

Alehoof, Gill-over-the-ground, Ground ivy
(Glechoma hederacea)

K, Kelly green

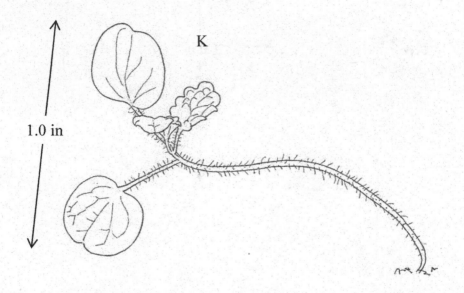

K

1.0 in

Bells-of-Ireland, Shellflower
(Moluccella laevis)

K, Kelly green

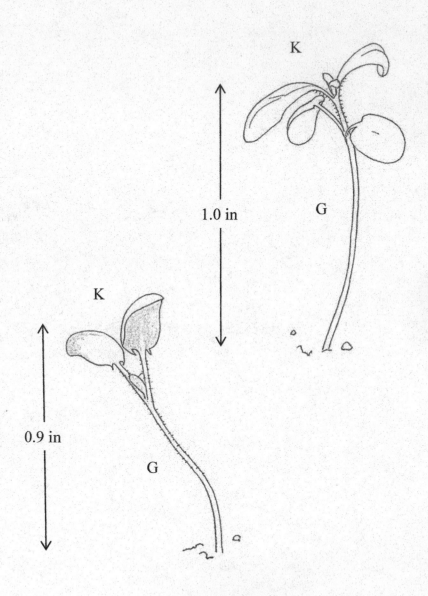

Rosemary
(Rosmarinus officinalis)

G, green tea; K, Kelly green

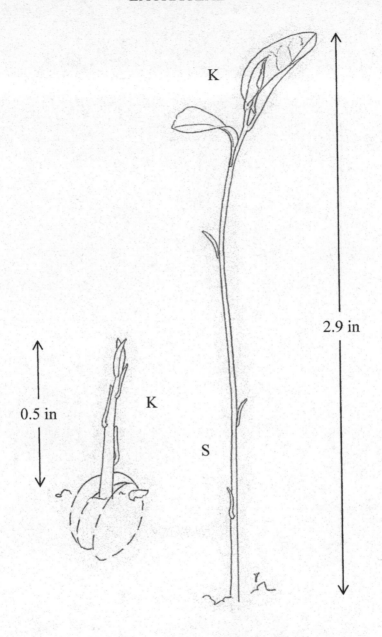

Spicebush, Wild allspice
(Lindera benzoin)

K, Kelly green; S, desert sand

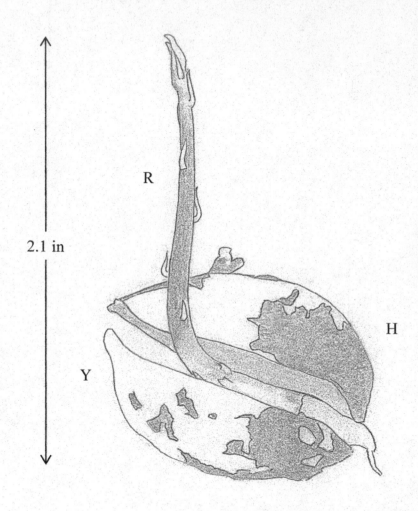

2.1 in

R

H

Y

Avocado
(Persea americana)

H, hickory brown; R, ruby red; Y, light yellow

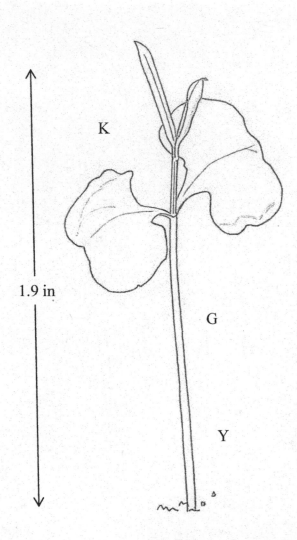

Pomegranate
(Punica granatum)

G, green tea; Kelly green; Y, light yellow

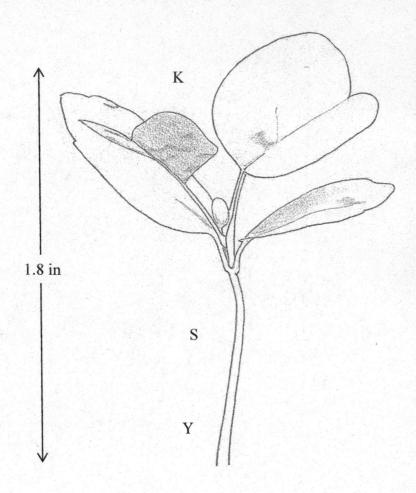

Tulip poplar, Tulip tree, Yellow-poplar
(Liriodendron tulipifera)

Kelly green; S, desert sand; Y, light yellow

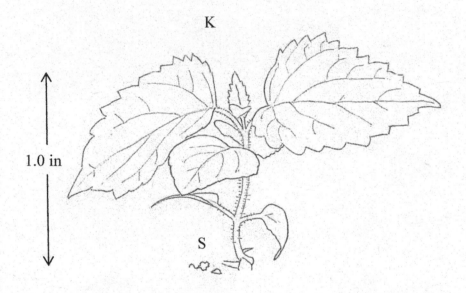

K

1.0 in

S

Buttonweed, Indian mallow, Velvetleaf
(Abutilon abutiloides)

K, Kelly green; S, desert sand

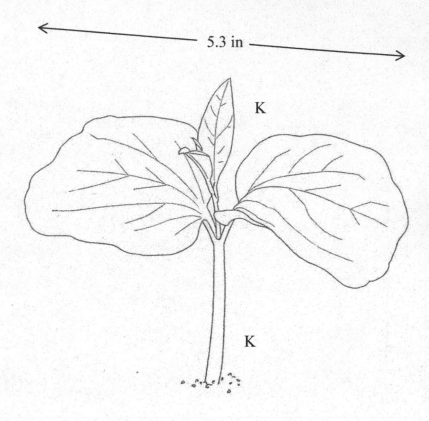

← —————— 5.3 in —————— →

K

K

African baobab, Monkey-bread tree
(Adansonia digitata)

K, Kelly green

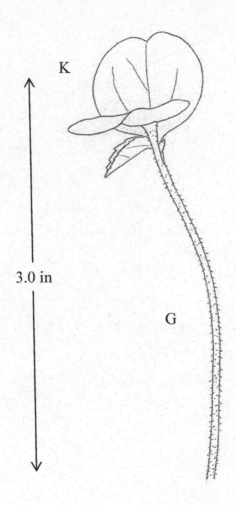

K

3.0 in

G

Ambary, Kenaf
(Hibiscus cannabinus)

G, green tea; K, Kelly green

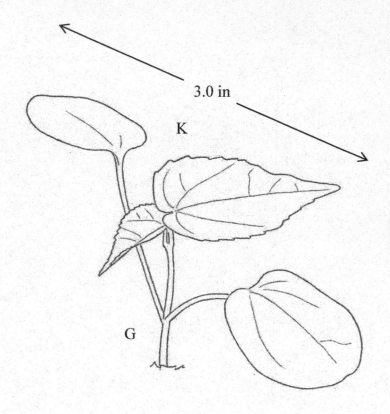

3.0 in

K

G

Scarlet rosemallow, Texas star
(Hibiscus coccineus)

G, green tea; K, Kelly green

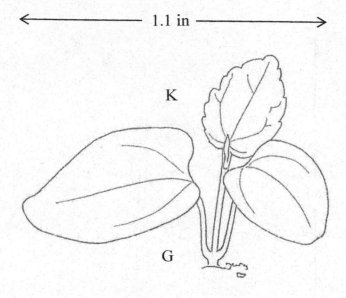

1.1 in

K

G

Eastern rosemallow, Swamp rose-mallow
(Hibiscus moscheutos 'palustris')

G, green tea; K, Kelly green

MALVACEAE

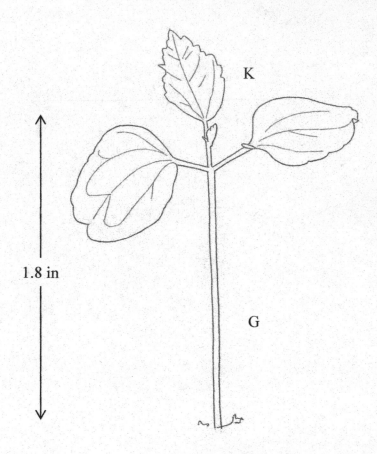

1.8 in

K

G

Rose of Sharon, Shrub althea
(Hibiscus syriacus)

G, green tea; K, Kelly green

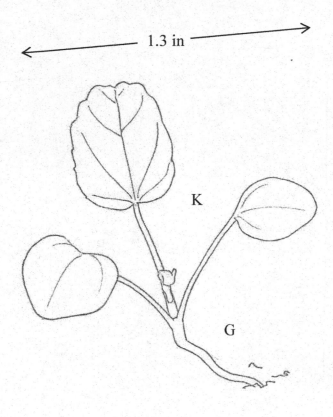

1.3 in

K

G

Bladder hibiscus, Flower-of-an-hour
(Hibiscus trionum)

G, green tea; K, Kelly green

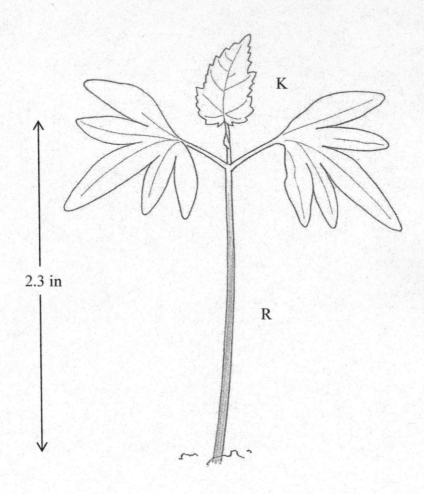

2.3 in

K

R

American basswood, American linden
(Tilia americana)

K, Kelly green; R, ruby red

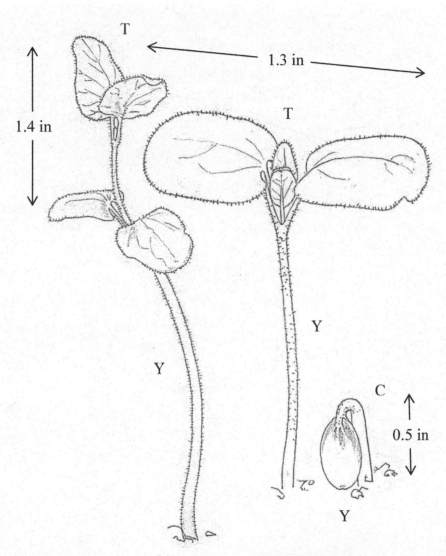

Devil's claw, Louisiana unicorn-plant, Ram's horn
(Proboscidea louisianica)

C, coral red; T, teal green; Y, light yellow

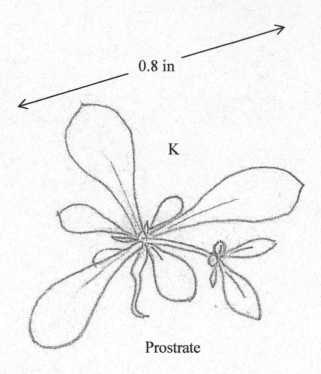

0.8 in

K

Prostrate

Green carpetweed, Indian chickweed
(Mollugo verticillata)

K, Kelly green

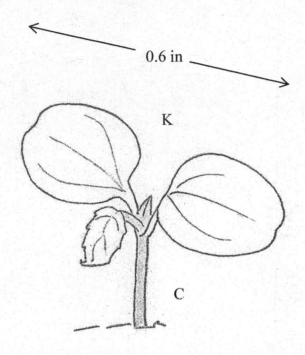

Congo fig
(Dorstenia elata)

C, coral red; K, Kelly green

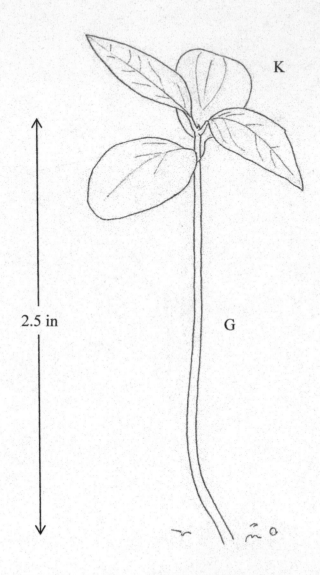

Horse apple, Mock orange, Osage orange
(Maclura pomifera)

G; green tea; K, Kelly green

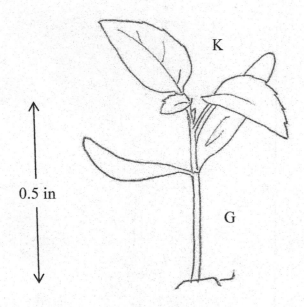

0.5 in

Silkworm mulberry, White mulberry
(Morus alba)

G, green tea; K, Kelly green

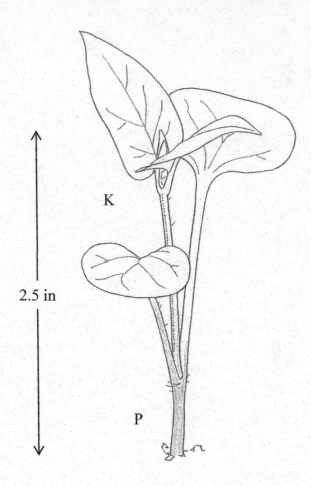

2.5 in

K

P

Four o'clock flower, Marvel of Peru
(Mirabilis jalapa)

K, Kelly green; P, light red

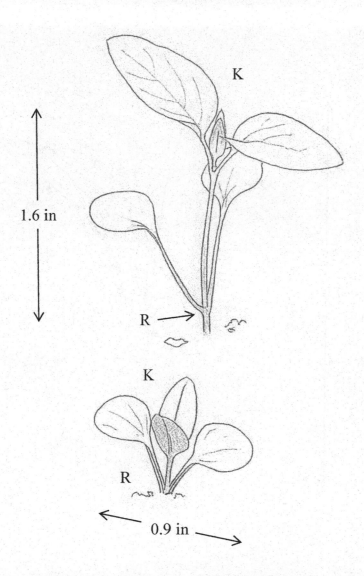

1.6 in

K

R →

K

R

← 0.9 in →

Heartleaf umbrella wort, Wild four o'clock
(Mirabilis nyctaginea)

K, Kelly green; R, ruby red

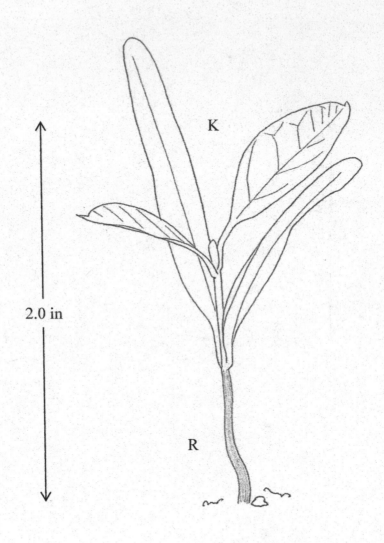

2.0 in

K

R

Green ash, Red ash, Swamp ash
(Fraxinus pennsylvanica)

K, Kelly green; R, ruby red

0.6 in

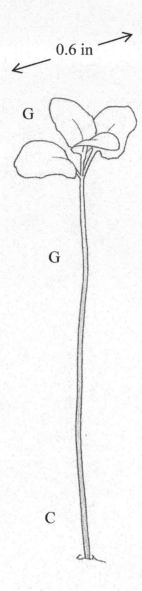

G

G

C

Farewell to spring, Rocky mountain garland
(Clarkia amoena)

C, coral red; G, green tea

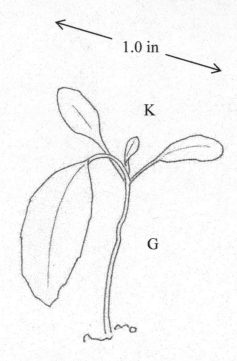

Common evening primrose, Evening star, Hog weed
(Oenothera biennis)

G, green tea; K, Kelly green

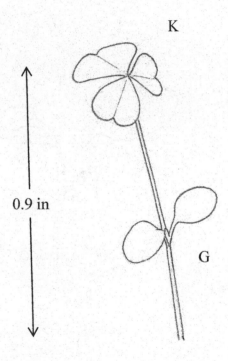

K

0.9 in

G

Common yellow woodsorrel, Lemon clover
(Oxalis stricta)

G, green tea; K, Kelly green

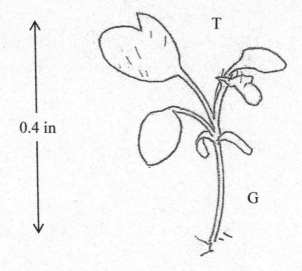

0.4 in

Pale poppy, Portage poppy
(Papaver alboroseum)

G, green tea; T, teal green

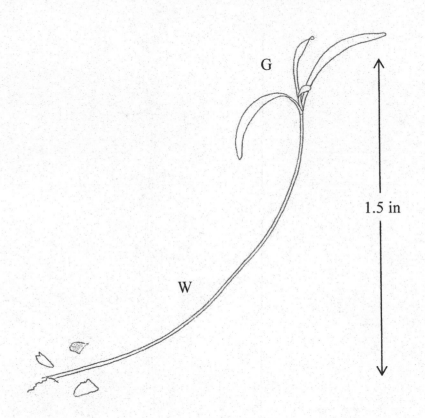

Breadseed poppy, Opium poppy
(Papaver somniferum)

G, green tea; W, white (and leggy)

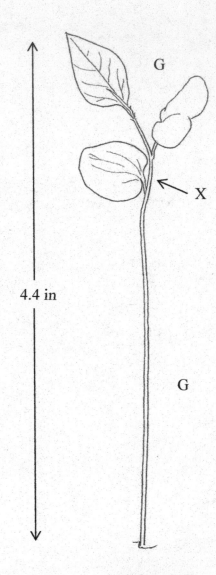

4.4 in

G

X

G

Passion flower, Passion vine
(Passiflora)

G, green tea; X, Alternating

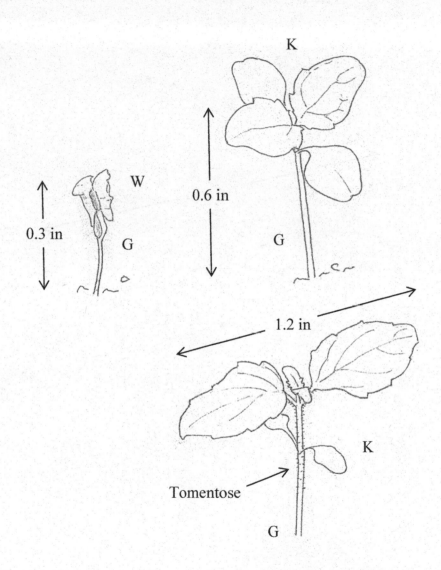

K

0.6 in

0.3 in

W

G

G

1.2 in

Tomentose

K

G

Empress tree, Princess tree
(Paulownia tomentosa)

G, green tea; K, Kelly green; W, white

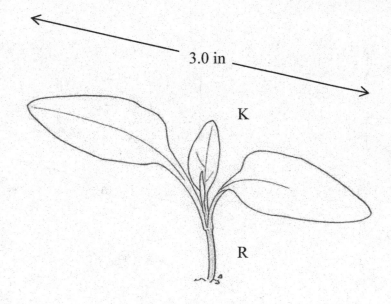

American pokeweed, Dragonberries, Inkberry
(Phytolacca americana)

K, Kelly green; R, ruby red

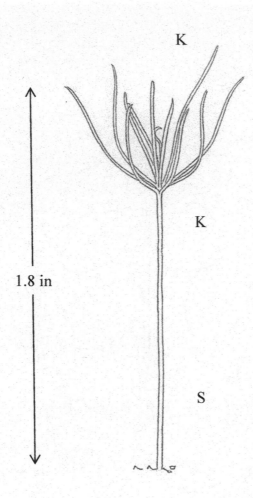

1.8 in

Eastern white pine, Weymouth pine
(Pinus strobus)

K, Kelly green; S, desert sand

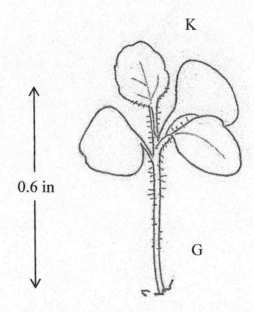

K

0.6 in

G

Common foxglove, Foxglove
(Digitalis purpurea)

G, green tea; K, Kelly green

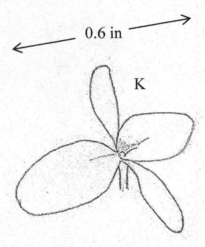

0.6 in

K

Broadleaf plantain, Waybread
(Plantago major)

K, Kelly green

PLATANACEAE

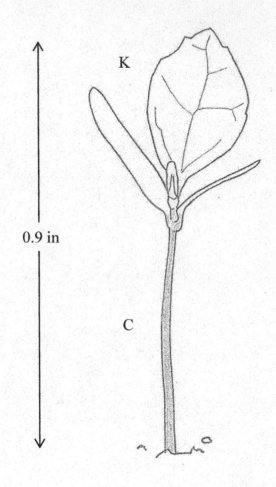

0.9 in

K

C

American planetree, Buttonwood, Sycamore
(Platanus occidentalis)

C, coral pink; K, Kelly green

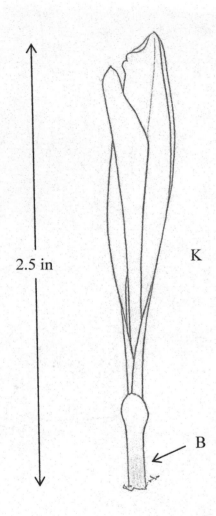

2.5 in

K

B

Corn, Maize
(Zea mays)

B, burgundy; K, Kelly green

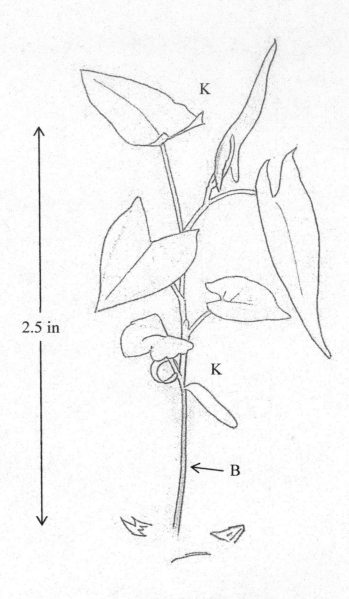

Black bindweed, Wild buckwheat
(Fallopia convolvulus)

B, burgundy; K, Kelly green

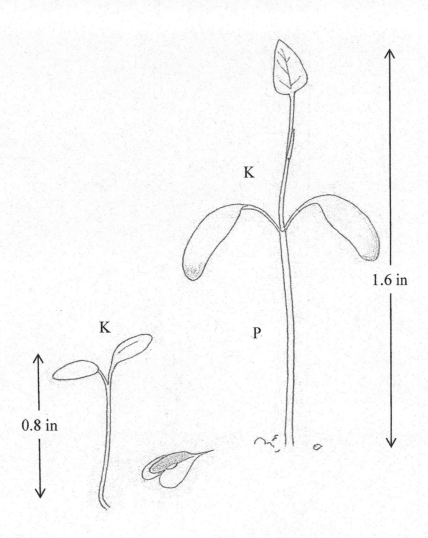

Asian knotweed, Japanese knotweed
(Reynoutria japonica)

K, Kelly green; P, light red

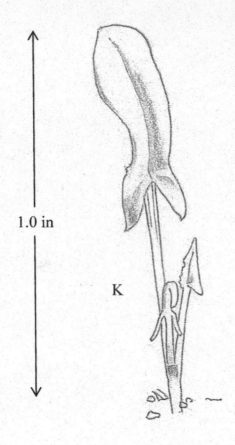

1.0 in

K

A root sprout

Red sorrel, Sheep's sorrel
(Rumex acetosella)

K, Kelly green

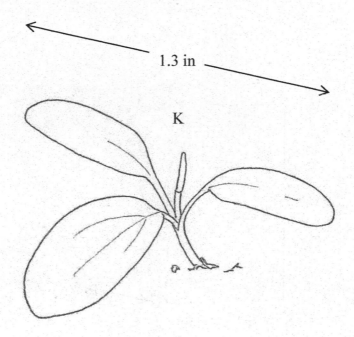

K

Curled dock, Yellow dock
(Rumex crispus)

K, Kelly green

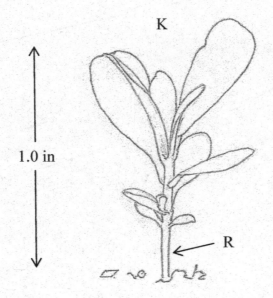

Common purslane, Little hogweed
(Portulaca oleracea)

K, Kelly green; R, ruby red

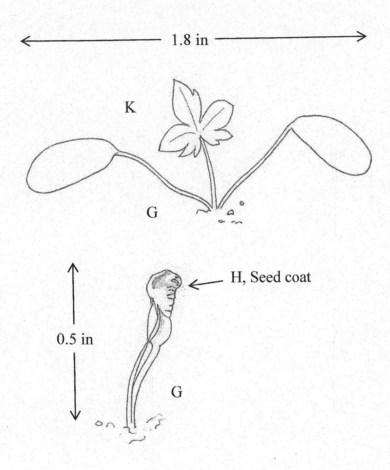

1.8 in

K

G

0.5 in

H, Seed coat

G

Aconite, Monk's-hood, Wolfsbane
(Aconitum napellus)

G, green tea; H, hickory brown; K, Kelly green

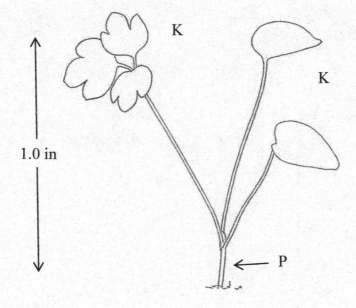

Crimson columbine, Western columbine
(Aquilegia formosa)

K, Kelly green; P, light red

← — 2.1 in — →

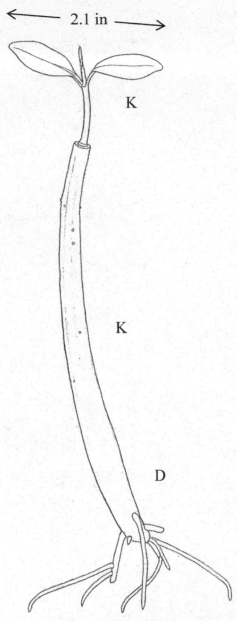

K

K

D

Red mangrove
(Rhizophora mangle)

D, desert sand; K, Kelly green

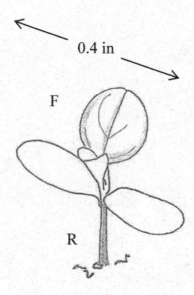

0.4 in

F

R

Cotoneaster 'Gnom', Willowleaf cotoneaster
(Cotoneaster salicifolius x gnom)

F, forest green; R, ruby red

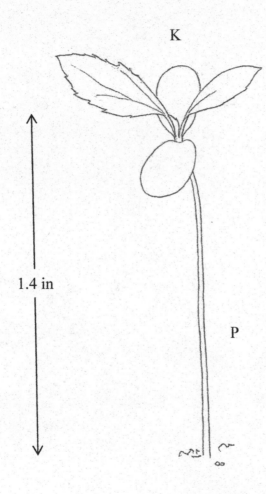

1.4 in

Hawthorn, May-tree, Quickthorn
(Crataegus)

K, Kelly green; P, light red

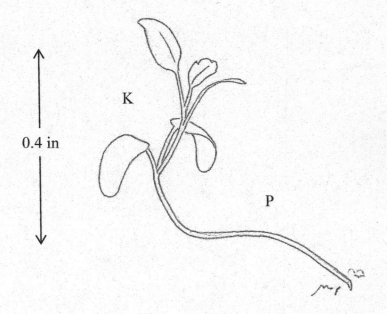

0.4 in

K

P

Yellow dryas, Yellow mountain-avens
(Dryas drummondii)

K, Kelly green; P, light red

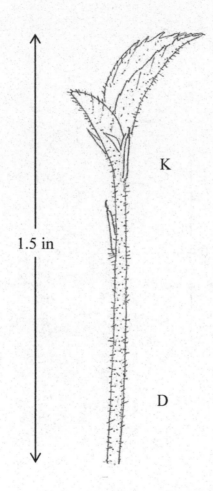

1.5 in

K

D

Loquat
(Eriobotrya japonica)

D, desert sand; K, Kelly green

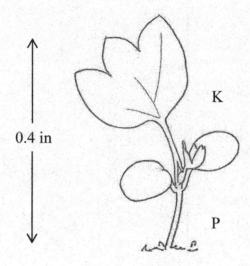

0.4 in

K

P

Garden strawberry, Strawberry
(Fragaria x ananassa)

K, Kelly green; P, light red

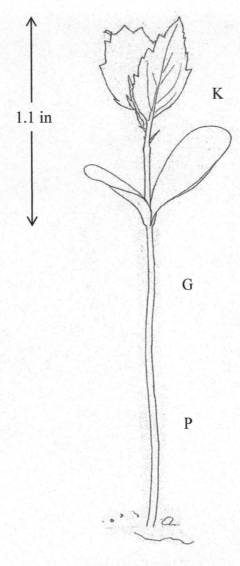

1.1 in

K

G

P

Apple
(Malus domestica)

G, green tea; K, Kelly green; P, light red

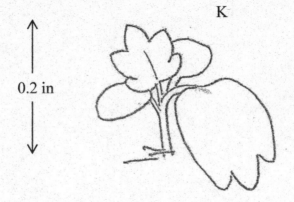

0.2 in

K

Dwarf cinquefoil
(Potentilla canadensis)

K, Kelly green

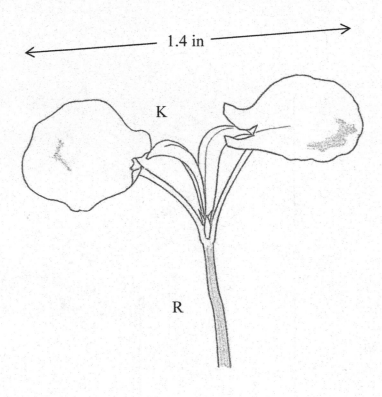

Cherry prinsepia, Chinese prinsepia
(Prinsepia sinensis)

K, Kelly green; R, ruby red

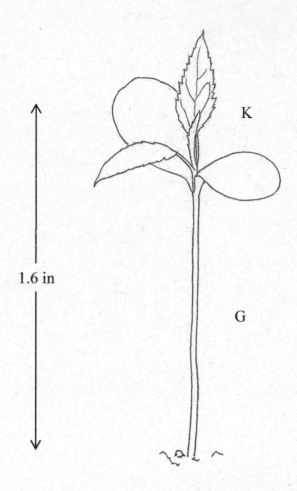

1.6 in

K

G

Allegheny plum
(Prunus alleghaniensis)

G, green tea; K, Kelly green

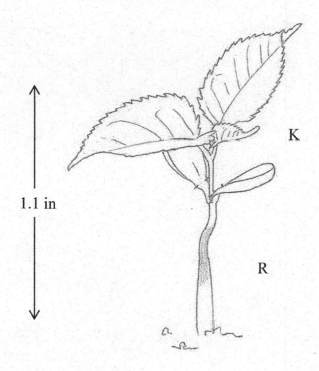

1.1 in

K

R

Bird Cherry, Fire Cherry, Pin cherry
(Prunus pensylvanica)

K, Kelly green; R, ruby red

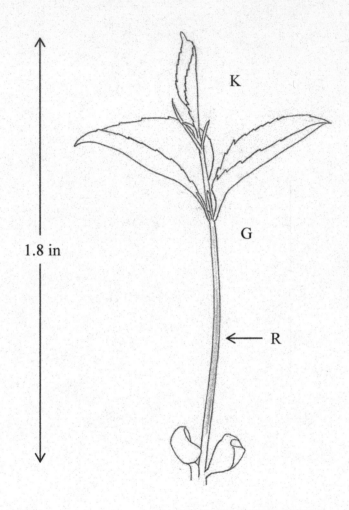

1.8 in

K

G

R

Black cherry, Wild black cherry
(Prunus serotina)

G, green tea; K, Kelly green; R, ruby red

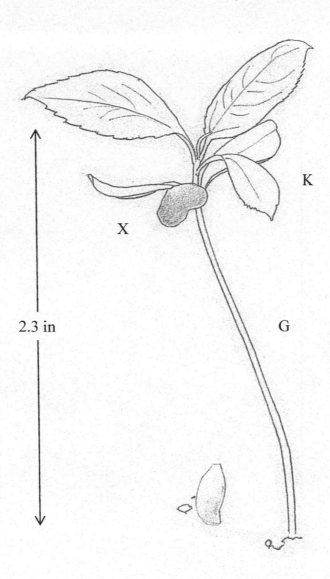

2.3 in

X

K

G

Common pear
(Pyrus communis)

G, green tea; K, Kelly green; X, rare third cotyledon

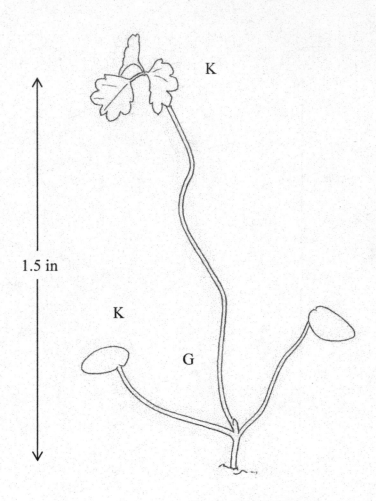

1.5 in

K

K

G

Great burnet
(Sanguisorba officinalis)

G, green tea; K, Kelly green

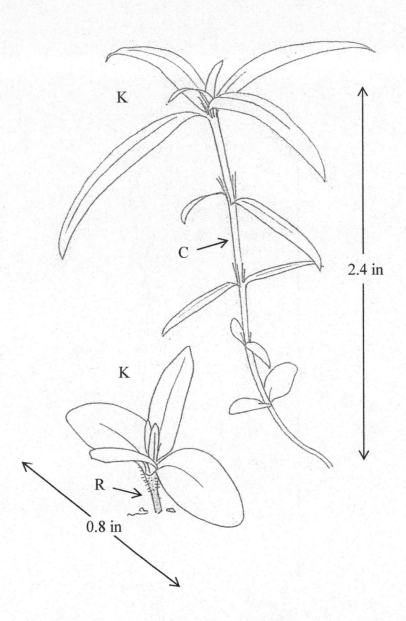

K

C →

2.4 in

K

R →

0.8 in

Poorjoe, Rough buttonweed
(Diodia teres)

C, coral pink; K, Kelly green; R, ruby red

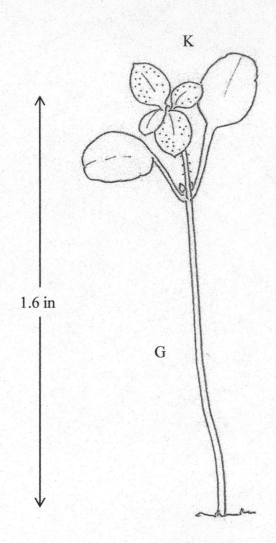

1.6 in

Catchweed, Cleavers, Sticky willy
(Galium aparine)

G, green tea; K, Kelly green

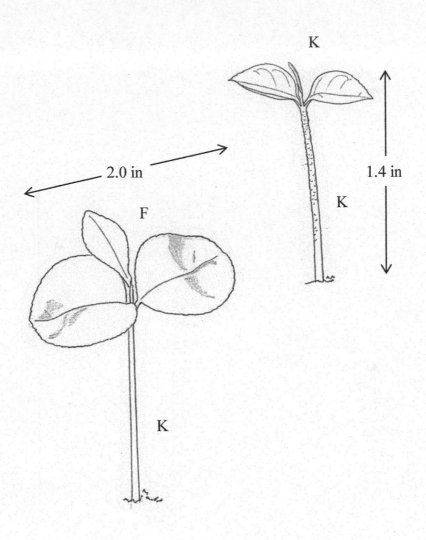

Grapefruit
(Citrus x paradisi)

F, forest green; K, Kelly green

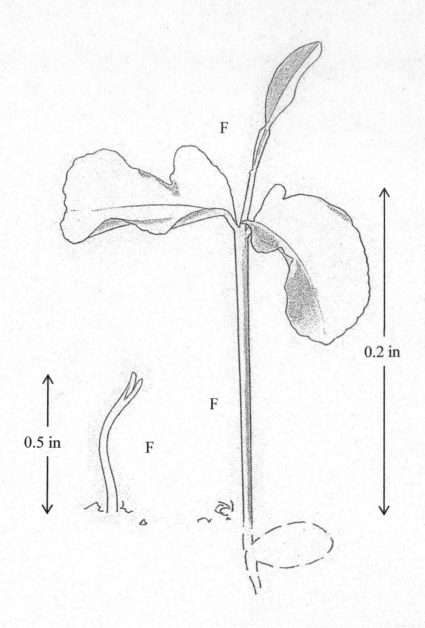

F

F

F

0.2 in

0.5 in

Sweet orange
(Citrus x sinensis)

F, forest green

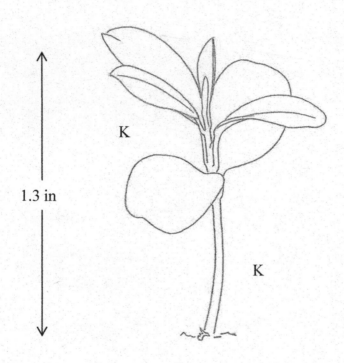

Japanese skimmia
(Skimmia japonica)

K, Kelly green

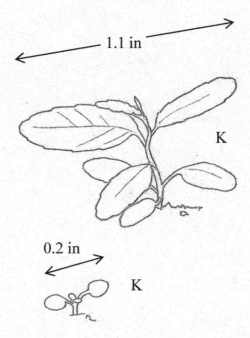

1.1 in

K

0.2 in

K

Black willow, Swamp willow
(Salix nigra)

K, Kelly green

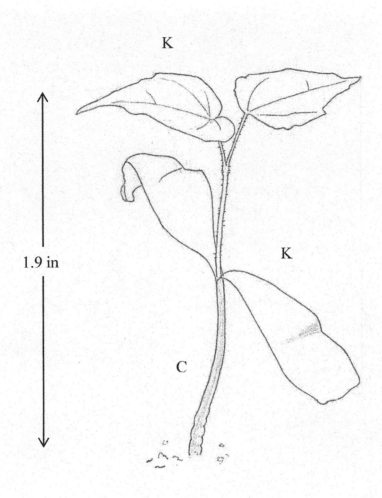

Paperbark maple
(Acer griseum)

C, coral red; K, Kelly green

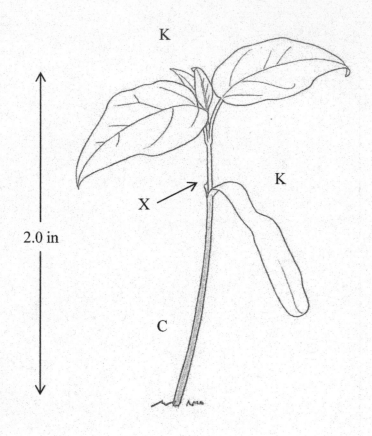

K

K

X

2.0 in

C

Boxelder maple, Manitoba maple
(Acer negundo)

C, coral red; K, Kelly green; X, Damaged

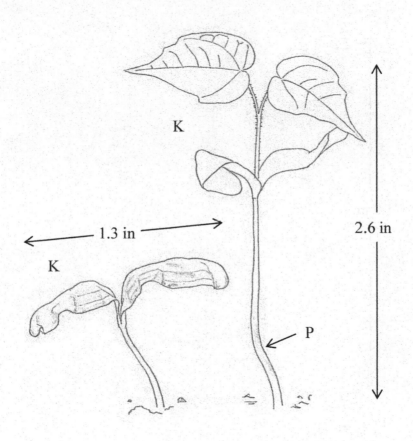

Norway maple
(Acer platanoides)

K, Kelly green; P, light red

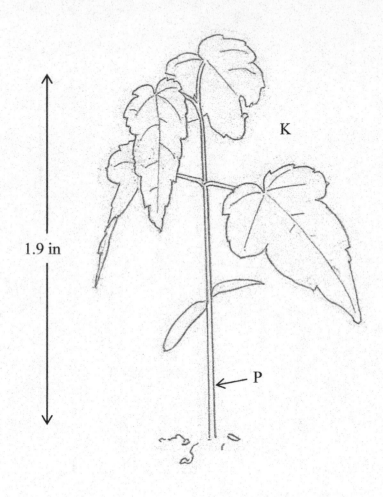

1.9 in

K

P

Red maple, Swamp maple, Water maple
(Acer rubrum)

K, Kelly green; P, light red

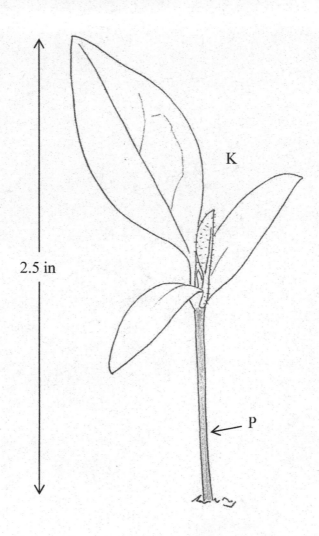

Aguay, Caimito, Star apple
(Chrysophyllum cainito)

K, Kelly green; P, light red

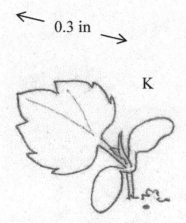

Astilbe, False spirea
(Astilbe x arendsii)

K, Kelly green

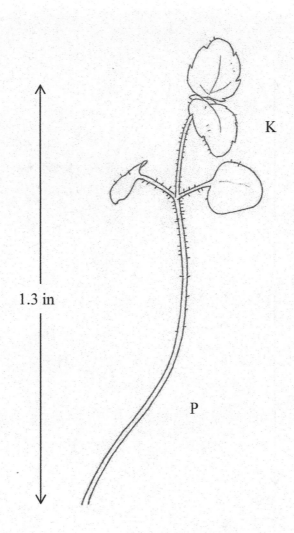

Mask flower, Scarlet mask flower
(Alonsoa Warscewiczii)

K, Kelly green; P, light red

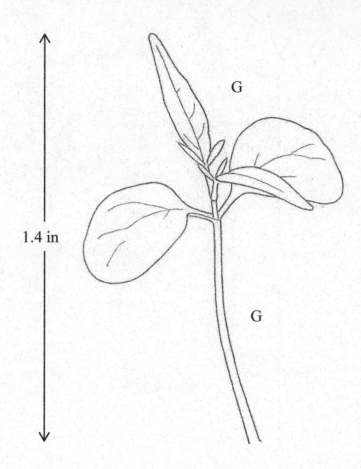

Tree of heaven, Varnish tree
(Ailanthus altissima)

G, green tea

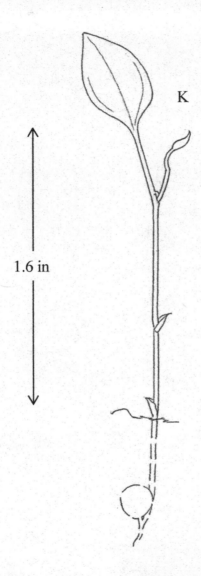

K

1.6 in

Common greenbrier, Roundleaf greenbriar
(Smilax rotundifolia)

K, Kelly green

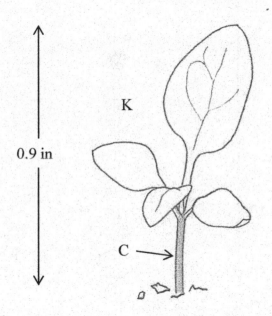

0.9 in

K

C →

Belladonna, Deadly nightshade
(Atropa belladonna)

C, coral pink; K, Kelly green

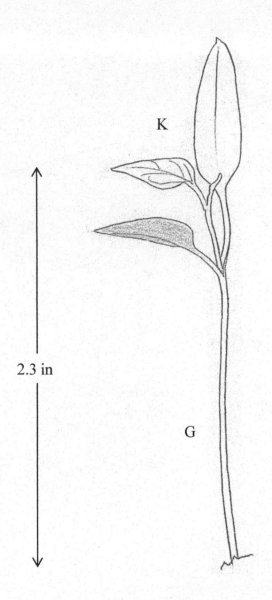

K

G

2.3 in

Pepper
(Capsicum annuum)

G, green tea; K, Kelly green

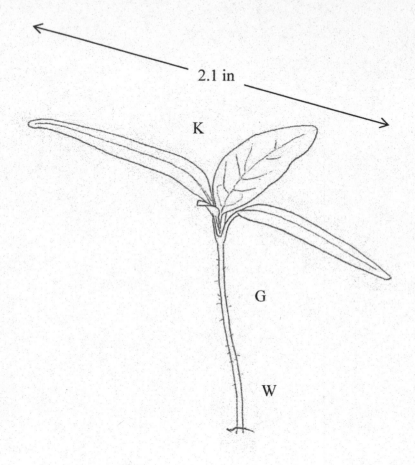

2.1 in

K

G

W

Devil's trumpet, Jimsonweed, Thorn apple
(Datura stramonium)

G, green tea; K, Kelly green; W, white

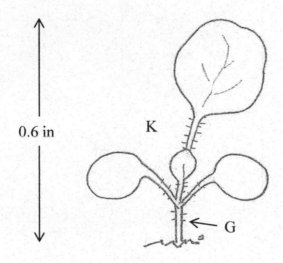

0.6 in

K

← G

Petunia
(Petunia x hybrida)

G, green tea; K, Kelly green

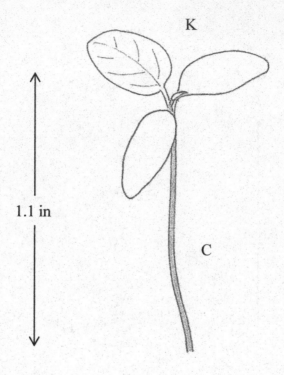

1.1 in

Carolina horsenettle, Radical weed, Sand brier
(Solanum carolinense)

C, coral pink; K, Kelly green

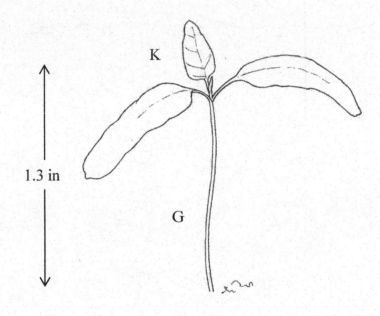

1.3 in

K

G

Bittersweet, Bittersweet nightshade, Blue bindweed
(Solanum dulcamara)

G, green tea; K, Kelly green

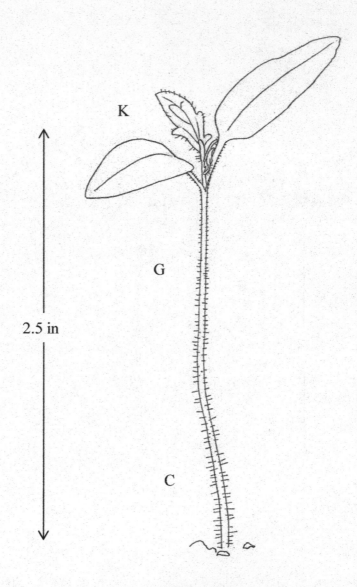

2.5 in

Tomato
(Solanum lycopersicum)

C, coral pink; G, green tea; K, Kelly green

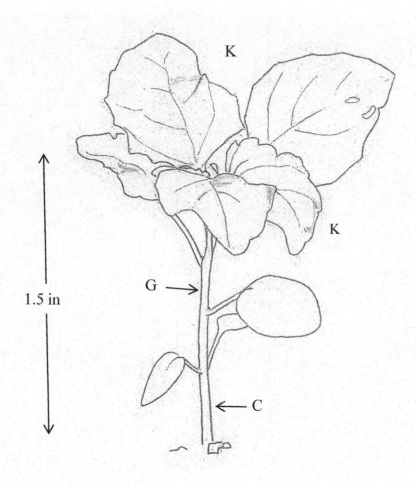

Black nightshade, Blackberry nightshade
(Solanum nigrum)

C, coral pink; G, green tea; K, Kelly green

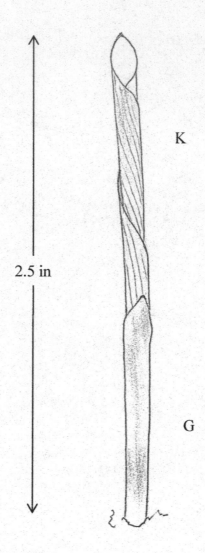

2.5 in

K

G

Giant white bird of paradise, Wild banana
(Strelitzia nicolai)

G, green tea; K, Kelly green

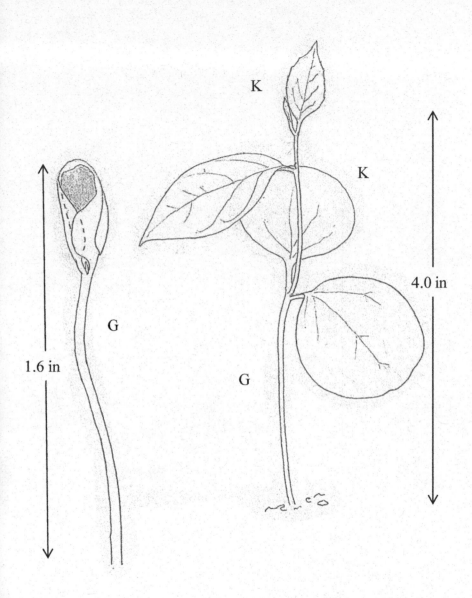

American snowbell, Mock-orange
(Styrax americanus)

G, green tea; K, Kelly green

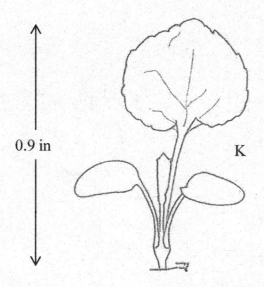

0.9 in

K

Broad-leaved wood violet
(Viola latiuscula)

K, Kelly green

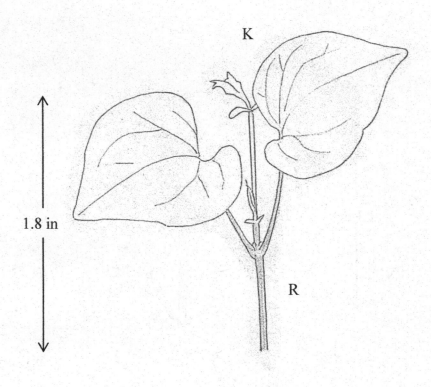

Five-leaved ivy, Virginia creeper, Woodbine
(Parthenocissus quinquefolia)

K, Kelly green; R, ruby red

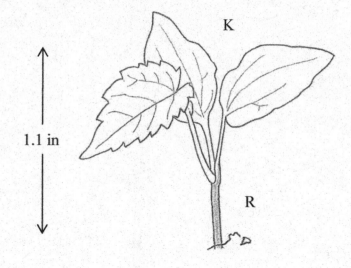

1.1 in

Pigeon grape, Summer grape
(Vitis aestivalis)

K, Kelly green; R, ruby red

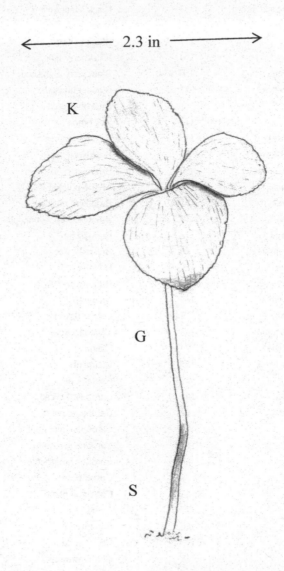

$\longleftarrow$ 2.3 in $\longrightarrow$

Cardboard cycad, Cardboard palm, Jamaican sago
(Zamia furfuracea)

G, green tea; K, Kelly green; S, desert sand

Index of Common Plant Names

Index of Common Plant Names

Index of Common Plant Names

Index of Common Plant Names

Index of Common Plant Names

One hundred and ninety seedling drawings, cataloged alphabetically by plant family name.

Features native and cultivated plants found growing throughout Northeast America.

Each is shown with a dimension and a color reference.

Contains an index to their common plant names.

'Mr. Taylor's work was of the highest caliber.'
- Charles P. Meidhof, P.E.

'His dedication to go over and above will be greatly missed.'
- Louis K. Robbins, P.E.

'Tom is a highly skilled AutoCADD technician and civil designer. He has an eye for detail and produces a high-quality set of plans.'
- Jay Hardman, P.E.